Faith Out Loud

A Cumberland Presbyterian
YOUTH RESOURCE
Volume 1, Quarter 1

Discipleship Ministry Team
Ministry Council
Cumberland Presbyterian Church

Revised
July 2017

8207 Traditional Place
Cordova (Memphis), Tennessee 38016

©2017 Discipleship Ministry Team

All Rights Reserved. No part of this book may be reproduced or transmitted in any form or by any means, electronic or mechanical, including photocopying, recording, or by any information storage or retrieval system, without permission in writing from the publisher with the single exception that purchase of this curriculum grants the purchaser the right to copy and distribute student handouts within each lesson for use in their local church. For information address Discipleship Ministry Team, Cumberland Presbyterian Center, 8207 Traditional Place, Cordova (Memphis), Tennessee, 38016-7414.

The Discipleship Ministry Team of the Ministry Council of the Cumberland Presbyterian Church is the successor organization to the Board of Christian Education of the Cumberland Presbyterian Church.

Funded, in part, by your contributions to Our United Outreach.

First Edition 2011
1st Revised Edition 2012
2nd Revised Edition 2017

Published by The Discipleship Ministry Team, CPC
Memphis, Tennessee

ISBN-13: 978-0615602455
ISBN-10: 0615602452

We want to hear from you.
Please send your comments about this curriculum to
the Discipleship Ministry Team at faithoutloud@cumberland.org

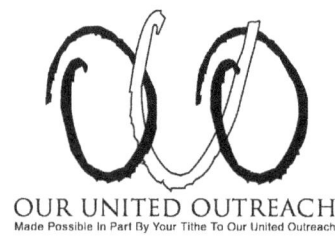

OUR UNITED OUTREACH
Made Possible In Part By Your Tithe To Our United Outreach

Table of Contents

Curriculum Users Guide v

Lesson 1: How Did We Get the Bible Anyway? 1

Lesson 2: FWIW: Getting the Most from Your Bible 13

Lesson 3: David and Goliath: Too Gory for a Kid's Story 27

Lesson 4: Good Kitty: Another Look at Daniel and Those Lions 39

Lesson 5: What's the Big Deal with the Big 10 51

Lesson 6: Is "Judgement House" Evangelism? 67

Lesson 7: Worship: BOOMM or GROOL? 81

Lesson 8: No Harm Done, It's Just for Fun! 95

Lesson 9: Job, Career, or Call: What's the Difference? 109

Lesson 10: Can Preachers Wear High Heels? 121

Lesson 11: Oops, We Made a Church! How the CP Church Was Born 135

Lesson 12: Are Christians Cannibals? A Look at Holy Communion 149

Lesson 13: Baby Showers: Baptism in the CP Church 161

Welcome to the Faith Out Loud curriculum!

It is our prayer that these lessons both encourage you and equip you as a youth leader—we're so grateful for what you do in the lives of students!

Blessings to you and your ministry!

Below are explanations of the components found in each lesson and tips for using this curriculum.

Lesson Title: Each lesson has a catchy title. Use these titles as teasers to get your students excited about upcoming gatherings.

Scripture: Each lesson has a key scripture reference. Spend some time studying and praying through each week's passage as you prepare to teach.

Theme: The theme statement gives you a quick snapshot into the main point of the lesson.

Before The Lesson: This section is usually divided into two parts: *Resource List* and *Leader Prep*. *Resource List* give you a quick list of all the stuff you need to gather for each week. *Leader Prep* give detailed instructions on the advance work that needs to be done for that week's activities. Do NOT wait until the night before you teach to review this section.

The Lesson: Once you move into the teaching time, you'll see these recurring elements:
- ✓ **Get Started:** These activities are designed to draw students into the material and set up the theme for the lesson.
- ✓ **Discussion Questions:** Usually a group of open-ended questions, these moments in the lesson are strategically placed to encourage your students to both think about and respond to the topic at hand.
- ✓ **Explain:** Placed in *italics*, these sections can be read verbatim to your students to help them fully understand the implications of the topic or theme. You'll discover you'll get the best response when you are thoroughly familiar with these sections and can deliver the same information in your own words instead of just reading the info to the students.
- ✓ **Leader Tips:** You'll find sections of side notes throughout each lesson. These are notes just for you, the leader. These notes offer you everything from instructions on how to facilitate the activities to background information on the subject to tips in making your lesson run smoothly.
- ✓ **Listen Up:** This section highlights a key scripture passage that should be read aloud. Encourage student to do these readings as often as possible.
- ✓ **Now What:** This section helps your students respond to the lesson. This will drive the lesson home and get your students thinking about the lesson in terms outside of the classroom walls.
- ✓ **Live It:** This is simply just the closing of each lesson, designed to help you conclude your time with your students well and offer them something to think about in the week ahead. Most weeks have handouts to pass along to your students during this time. You may find it helpful to encourage your students to get a folder to keep these handouts together so they can easily refer to them during the week.
- ✓ **Handouts:** At the end of each week's lesson, you'll find a reproducible page. Your purchase of this curriculum grants you the right to print and distribute copies to everyone in your group.

"How Did We Get the Bible Anyway?"
By Andy McClung

Scripture: Hebrews 4:12-13; 2 Timothy 3:15-17

Theme: This lesson tells the story of how the scriptures developed from the time of their writings, to canonization, and to contemporary English translations.

Resource List

- One set of 66 index cards for every eight students.
- An opaque bag big enough to hold a Bible discretely
- Any translation Bible with a table of contents
- Seven sheets of newsprint, poster board, butcher paper or giant sticky notes and a way to hide or cover them until they are needed.
- A marker
- Copy "Bible Timeline" handout for each student.
- (Optional) Writing samples of Hebrew, Aramaic, and Greek; just a few letters or some simple words. Hebrew and Greek characters may be in your processing program's symbols, and all three alphabets are on Wikipedia.

Leader Prep

- For the opening activity, find an open space appropriate for lots of movement and shouting, and as free of wind as possible. Mark it off into equal-sized territories. You'll need one territory per eight students in your group.
- For each set of 66 index cards, print one book of the Bible on each card. You'll need one set of index cards per 8 students in your group.
- Using the seven giant sheets of paper, make the following signs and then keep these quotes covered or hidden until you're ready to use them:

1. The Lord gouerneth me, and no thing to me shal lacke; in the palce of leswe where he me ful sette. Ouer water of fulfilling he nurshide me; my soule he conuertide.
2. Our Lord ruleth me, and nothing shal be wanting to me: inplace of pasture there he hath placed me. Upon the water of refection he hath brought me up; he hath conuerted my soule.
3. The LORD is my shepherd, I lack nothing. He makes me lie down in green pastures, he leads me beside quiet waters, he refreshes my soul.
4. God lufede middan-eard swa þæt he sealde hys akennedan sune þæt nan ne for-wurðe þe on hine ge-lefð. Ac habbe þt eche lyf.
5. For God so loued the worlde, that he gaue his onely sonne, that who so euer beleueth in hi, shulde not perishe, but haue euerlastinge life.
6. For God so loved the world that he gave his one and

1

Notes:

only Son, that whoever believes in him shall not perish but have eternal life.
7. Leave the last one blank
- Pray for your students and yourself as you prepare to lead this lesson.

 ## Leader Insights

Connecting to Your Students
Just as we need to prepare the resources for a lesson, we need to prepare our hearts and minds for the Biblical and theological insights each lesson provides. Familiarize yourself with these insights to help you respond to the discussion questions and activities throughout the lesson.

LI#1: We are accustomed to books having just one author, but the Bible has around 40 writers who wrote at different times, for different reasons, in different styles, and for different audiences over a span of almost two thousand years. We say 'about 40 writers' because we're not completely sure who wrote every single book of the Bible, and some books appear to have had more than one writer. Instead of calling the Bible a book, it may be more accurate to call it a library.

LI#2: We call the Bible "the word of God,' because it's God's message—or word—to us. It is important to note that the Bible never calls itself "the word of God." Several Bible verses refer to scripture, like 2 Timothy 3:15-17, but no verse was written with the whole Bible, as we know it today, in mind. This is simply because the Bible as we know it today wasn't compiled when any of it was being written. Even so, we understand that verses referring to scripture typically refer to the whole Bible. We often call it simply 'The Bible', but it's actually 'The Holy Bible.' The word 'bible' comes from the Greek and just means 'book.' The word 'holy' means something set apart by God for a sacred purpose. 'The Holy Bible,' then, means 'the holy book.' It's called 'Bible' because it's a book, and it's called 'Holy' because it's about God. More precisely, the Bible is the story of God's relationship with humankind."

Some people who want to discredit Christianity point to the fact that no original manuscripts of the Bible exist. That's true: The best we have are copies of copies of copies of copies, and most of those are just portions of the various books of the

Bible. What is amazing, though, is that whenever an ancient manuscript is newly discovered, we see that those who hand-copied the scriptures over the centuries were pretty accurate. We have over 13,000 partial manuscripts from different sources, some of which are over 2,000 years old, but most of which are just hundreds of years old. When differences are found between ancient sources, scholars decide which manuscript is more likely to be closest to the original. The oldest complete Bible we have is the *Codex Vaticanus*, which was put together in first half of the Fourth Century.

This lesson covers how the Bible came to be and may answer and open up questions your students have about the Bible.

Explaining the Bible

Some people think that God simply handed the Bible—in completed form—to King James in 1611. Humans actually were very much involved in the development of the Bible, but that doesn't diminish God's involvement in guiding the process. Some people say God dictated the Bible, making humans write exactly what God wanted them to. Others say God inspired humans to write what they did; God gave them the ideas and they put it in their own words. Others say humans wrote the Bible in response to what they saw God doing in the world. The truth is, the Bible may be partially each of those, but it's not any one of them alone.

The oldest stories in the Bible were told and retold for generations without any changes to the stories. It's hard for us to understand this way of keeping history because we can't even go around a circle without changing one simple sentence. But whispering from person to person is not how biblical stories were passed along in ancient times. It was more like when we learned to recite the Pledge of Allegiance or the Lord's Prayer. Biblical stories were verbally passed along by one person teaching them to a group, and repeating them frequently. If there were any mistakes or omissions in the telling, someone in the audience would correct the speaker. With all the technology available to us today, we don't have to remember much of anything. So, while we may not be very good at verbally passing along stories without changing them, ancient peoples were very good at it. With the lack of easily accessible ink and paper, they had to be.

As ink and paper and the art of writing developed, these biblical stories were written down. First they would have been written on leather or papyrus. Papyrus was thick, rough paper

Books Scramble Leader Tips:

1. Small group? Make smaller teams. Have a very small group? Play with just one team.

2. If you have a student or two in your group who happens to know the Bible well enough to complete the task, then let the game run its course.

3. Decide before the game starts whether or not to allow the use of smart phones. If allowed, don't mention it and see how long it takes somebody to think of it. If not allowed, say so up front.

4. Wait until someone asks for help (or until a team seems to be on the verge of giving up) before you reveal the Bible you brought along and offer it for their use. Keep the Bible in a central location and have the students come to it rather than take it back to their game territory.

5. If no one has thought of using a smart phone, you might suggest using one as well.

6. You might joke about how hard this is, or wonder aloud if even the pastor could do it.

Leader Tip:

You probably have in your church some sweet, grey-haired lady who knows the Bible thoroughly. Even she, however, may not understand how the Bible came to be. Your church's young adults and students may, in fact, be more aware than the seasoned citizens as to how we got the Bible because of recent media attention to the so-called "lost" or "secret" books of the Bible. Discussing the development of the Bible makes some Christians uncomfortable. This may be because they hold the Bible in such high esteem they don't like to think about humans being overly involved in the process, or there could be another reason. If this comes up be sure to see "Just in Case" at the end of the lesson.

---

made from the spongy insides of a plant. The papyrus was made into long scrolls up to twenty-four feet long. Papyrus doesn't last very long, so copies were made by hand when a scroll began to wear out. Extreme care was taken to ensure that every word and letter was copied exactly.

Over the years, the Bible has been translated into many different languages so people of all nations can understand it. The first time was in 285 B.C., translating the Old Testament into Greek. This was done primarily for those Jewish people who lived outside of Israel and no longer spoke Hebrew. The result is called The Septuagint. The next translation was taking the original Hebrew and Greek and translating them into Latin. The result is called the Vulgate and was completed in A.D. 400. The first translation into English was in 1384, but we'd hardly recognize it as English today.

The various books of the New Testament were used for many decades before anybody decided that there needed to be an official canon. When a bunch of other writings started showing up with claims to be additional writings of Jesus and his disciples, some of which had teachings contrary to what was in the verifiable scriptures, the church leaders took action and set the canon as the twenty-seven books we know today. Their decisions about which writings to include in the canon were based on how closely the writer was connected to Jesus and how effective the writing had been in the church already. So, a writing claiming to be the words of one of the disciples but clearly written over a hundred years after his death and which had done little to draw people to Christ or deepen believers' faith was not considered. Some books were easy to decide about (Matthew, Mark, Acts, most of Paul's letters), some were the subject of much debate (James, Revelation) but made it in, and some were dismissed.

No scripture was originally written to include chapters and verses, but over the years different methods were used to make finding specific passages easier. There is some debate over exactly who added the currently used chapter and verse numbers and when it happened, but it was probably between the 1200s and the 1500s.

Theological Underpinnings

The Book Scramble and Gossip activities will help your students begin thinking about the process that produced the Bible as we know it today, and the Bible study will lead them in beginning to explore that process. Helping your students understand that the Bible is the most amazing book that's ever existed is a one of the greatest gifts you can give them: it's the story of God's interaction with humankind, from the moment God created us through what God will do in the future. Despite how many people have had a hand in writing, editing, copying, and translating the Bible, God has made sure that it still remains holy, and "the authoritative guide for Christian living" (*Confession of Faith* 1.05).

Applying the Lesson to Your own Life
What's your earliest memory of the Bible? When was the first time you remember wondering about where the Bible came from and how it was put together? Who is the person you know or remember as being the most knowledgeable about the Bible? Who is the person you know or remember who could most bring the Bible to life? Did you memorize the books of the Bible as a child? Can you still say, or sing, them?

Many pastors fail to spend time reading the Bible outside of sermon or teaching preparation. Do you spend time "in" the Bible outside of preparing for class?

What's you favorite book of the Bible? Why is it your favorite? Do you know who wrote it? Do you know to whom it was originally written? Do you know what was going on in the world at the time it was written? Do you know if it there was debate about including it in the canon? Consider spending the next few months finding out all you can about your favorite book.

The Lesson

Get Started (15 min.)

Books Scramble

Take with you one set of Bible books printed index cards for each team and the bag containing the Bible and lead your students to the activity zone already marked.

Divide your group into equal teams of about eight.

Direct each team to its territory and hold up a stack of index

Media Option:

The Book of Eli is a powerful movie representation of God's word. The world has almost been destroyed and Eli is charged with carrying the last copy of the Bible all the way across the country and to protect it. People seek to get it because they hear that it has power and they want that power for selfish reasons. The movie is rated R and cannot be shown in its entirety, but you might consider showing the movie trailer and then showing the concluding clip to the movie when Eli recites the Bible.

Notes:

cards and explain what it is. Explain that the teams will race to see which team can be the first to put the cards in their correct order. (If you have only one team, say they're racing against the clock and have five minutes to complete the task.)

Throw the cards into each team's territory, causing the cards to scatter randomly, and give your "go" signal.

When one team claims to have completed the task, the other teams get to continue working while you verify the win. Once you have a confirmed winner, have members of the winning team loudly call out the books, in correct order.
The winning team gets to clean up all the cards and whatever you used to mark off territories.

Discussion Questions:
- How hard was this task?
- What sections of the Bible did you think you knew?
- How many Christians do you know who could complete this task?

Transition: *The Bible really is a "Book of books" and today we're going to learn about how the Bible came to be.*

 # Listen Up (20-25 min.)

READ: Have someone read aloud 2 Timothy 3:15-17.

Discussion Questions:
- What's your favorite book, and who wrote it?
- What are some other ways we refer to the Bible besides, "the Bible"?

Gossip

Play a quick game of Gossip, also known as Whisper, Telephone, or Secret Message. To play, have everyone form a circle and a selected player starts by whispering a secret message—only once—into the ear of the player to his or her left. That player whispers the message—only once—into the ear of the player to his or her left, and so on until the message has been passed all the way around the circle. The last player says aloud what he or she heard and then the first player says aloud the original message. The result is often funny because the message usually changes during its journey around the circle. To ensure a laugh, you may want to originate the message and make it nonsensical (e.g. "The monkey likes to wear purple mittens in the spring") or poke fun at yourself (e.g. "<your name>'s feet smell like rotten cantaloupes.") Move on with the lesson after the game.

Discussion Questions:
- How many phone numbers or addresses do you know by heart—without looking at your phone?
- How do you find numbers when you need them?

Say: Your parents and grandparents had to memorize phone numbers, but we don't anymore because our cell phones remember them for us. In the same way, ancient peoples used to have to memorize their own history, but then they moved to writing it.

English, Please?

Expose newsprint sheet #1 and ask somebody to read it out loud. Then do the same with sheet #2. Reveal that they're the same Bible passage and ask if anyone recognizes it. They are both Psalm 23:1-2, sheet #1 is from the Wycliffe Bible, A.D. 1384, and sheet #2 is from the Douai Old Testament, A.D. 1609. Uncover sheet #3 which is the same passage from a recent translation (TNIV).

Repeat this process with sheets #4-6. Sheet #4 is John 3:16 from an English translation made around A.D. 1200. Sheet #5 is from the Coverdale Bible, A.D. 1535. Sheet #6 is from a recent translation (TNIV).

Say: *All these are in English, but some sure don't look like it, do they?*

Discussion Questions:
- What are some words or phrases your parents or grandparents use that may as well be a foreign language?

Write responses until you've used about half of sheet #7.

- What are some words or phrases you use that probably won't make any sense to your kids or grandkids?

Notes:

Just in Case:

Apocryphal Books

Some of your students may be interested in the Apocryphal books which Roman Catholics include as scripture and we do not. In 1548, at the Council of Trent, the Roman Catholic Church affirmed some extra books as scripture. Since this was after the Reformation had begun, the Protestant church didn't adopt these extra books.

Other writings exist which some say should be in the Bible. These are sometimes called "lost" or "secret" books, or perhaps the Gnostic gospels. Most of them were written well after the canonized books and have dubious authenticity.

Use the rest of sheet #7 to write some of these.

Say: *Language changes over time, which is why scholars continue to study and translate the original languagesof the Bible into contemporary language. Originally, the Old Testament was written mostly in Hebrew. Parts of Ezra, Jeremiah, and Daniel were written in Aramaic. The New Testament was written in Greek, with a few Aramaic phrases thrown in.*

Over the years, the Bible has been translated into many different languages so people of all nations can understand it. The first time was in 285 B.C., translating the Old Testament into Greek. This was done primarily for those Jewish people who lived outside of Israel and no longer spoke Hebrew. The result is called The Septuagint. The next translation was taking the original Hebrew and Greek and translating them into Latin. The result is called the Vulgate and was completed in A.D. 400. The first translation into English was in 1384, but we'd hardly recognize it as English today—remember the 'English' versions we just looked at?

Discussion Questions:
- Since the Bible is made up of all these different books written over all those centuries, does anyone know who put it all together into the form we have now, and when?
- Does anyone know what a 'canon' has to do with any of this?

Explain: B*esides being that thing on the side of a pirate ship that goes boom, a 'canon' is also a set of writings which have been officially recognized as genuine. Once a canon is recognized (or completed), no other books are to be added to it; the canon is fixed or closed. We're not exactly sure when the Old Testament was canonized. Some scholars believe that Ezra (from the Old Testament) put it together five hundred years before Jesus was born. What we do know is that a historian, Josephus, mentions the Old Testament as we know it in A.D. 95 and says that this canon had been fixed for hundreds of years.*

Share: *The various books of the New Testament were used for many decades before anybody decided that there needed to be an official canon. When a bunch of other writings started showing up with claims to be additional writings of*

Jesus and his disciples, some of which had teachings contrary to what was in the verifiable scriptures, the church leaders took action and set the canon as the twenty-seven books we know today. Their decisions about which writings to include in the canon were based on how closely the writer was connected to Jesus and how effective the writing had been in the church already. So, a writing claiming to be the words of one of the disciples but clearly written over a hundred years after his death and which had done little to draw people to Christ or deepen believers' faith was not considered. Some books were easy to decide about (Matthew, Mark, Acts, most of Paul's letters), some were the subject of much debate (James, Revelation) but made it in, and some were dismissed.

Discussion Question:
- If the Bible wasn't written all at once, how did they know how to put in numbers for the chapters and verses?

Explain: *No scripture was originally written to include chapters and verses, but over the years different methods were used to make finding specific passages easier. There is some debate over exactly who added the currently used chapter and verse numbers and when it happened, but it was probably between the 1200s and the 1500s.*

Now What? (10-15 min.)

Discussion Question:
- Now that you know the story of how we got the Bible, what do you think?

In conclusion, help your students understand that the Bible is the most amazing book that has ever existed. It's the story of God's interaction with humankind, from the moment God created us through what God will do in the future. People have dedicated their lives to copying and preserving it. People have risked their lives to gain access to it. People have given up their lives to share it. How we got Bibles that are so plentiful and familiar in our lives is an incredible story covering thousands of years.

Clearly, God wants us to have this book. Even if you take God

Notes:

Notes:

completely out of the picture, even if you think the Bible is a bunch of baloney, you have to admit that the Bible is a miracle. When one considers how old it is, how it developed, and how it has been preserved, one can't help but affirm that the Bible is absolutely unique: there's no other book like it in the world.

 ## Live It (5 min.)

Have the group join you in prayer.

Prayer: *Thank you God, for this book we call the Bible. Thank you for inspiring men and women to write it, to preserve, to translate it, and to teach us about it. Amen.*

Give each student a Bible timeline handout and a Bible to students who do not own one.

Encourage students to ask their parents about their favorite scripture and book of the Bible.

© 2011 Discipleship Ministry Team of the Ministry Council of the Cumberland Presbyterian Church, All Rights Reserved.

Bible Timeline

The Bible is a library of 66 books: 39 in the Old Testament; 27 in the New Testament.

1400 to 400 B.C.
The Old Testament is written, recording both the stories that have already been passed down verbally for generations and the new stuff that is happening.

285 B.C.
The Old Testament is translated from Hebrew into Greek.

A.D. 45 to 90.
The New Testament is written, recording both what's already happened the gospels and some of Acts) and the new stuff that is happening. James may have been the first book written, Revelation was probably the last book written.

A.D. 95.
Josephus, an historian, identifies the Old Testament canon as the 39 books we know and says they'd been accepted for hundreds of years.

A.D. 397.
The Council of Carthage (a meeting of church leaders) officially affirms the 27 books of the New Testament.

A.D. 400.
The whole Bible is translated into Latin: The Vulgate. Latin was the predominate language used for the next several centuries.

A.D. 1384
The first English translation of the Bible is completed: the Wycliffe Bible.

A.D. 1456
The Vulgate is printed on a printing press with moveable type: the Gutenberg Bible.

A.D. 1526
William Tyndale prints the New Testament and part of the Old Testament in English so everyone can have access to them. He is later executed for doing so.

A.D. 1535
First complete Bible mechanically printed in English: the Coverdale Bible.

A.D. 1611
King James 1 of England has a team produce an English version of the entire Bible: the King James Version or the Authorized Version.

A.D. 1885
A group of scholars, using manuscripts not previously available, produce the Revised Version.

A.D. 1966 to 1979
New versions are produced, including the NIV in 1979, translating the scripture into contemporary English.

Today there are many different translations in English, and translations into other contemporary languages continue. Some dates above are approximate.

FWIW:
Getting the Most from Your Bible
By Andy McClung

Scripture: 2 Timothy 3:16-17

Theme: Students are often told to read their Bibles, but are seldom taught how to do so effectively.

Resource List

- An assortment of pens, notebooks, pads, paper, crayons, markers, colored pencils
- One copy per student of the "John 7:53-8:11" handout
- One copy per student of the "Bible Study Guide" handout

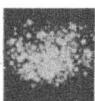

Leader Prep

In this lesson, students will get a chance to try out some interactive Bible study methods. For students to get the most out of this lesson, it is important that this meeting begins calmly. Ensure your meeting space is as quiet and physically comfortable as possible.

Here are some was to help to insure this:
- Announce it in advance and offer a special reward if things go smoothly.
- Call or visit high-energy students and let them know this week's lesson will be different.
- Ask several adults to sit in to help keep things calm. (Remember: calmness breeds calmness. Choose calm adults and be at your calmest, too.)
- If your gathering time is usually loud or physically active, arrange to gather somewhere else until all have arrived and then calmly move as a group to your meeting space or use a different space this week.
- Collect phones and store them in another room for this meeting, or make everyone turn them off. (Off, not silenced.)
- Create enough space for each student to have privacy
- Eliminate any other distracting noise sources.
- Reduce lighting by half by covering windows or bringing in lamps instead of overhead fluorescents
- Have a scented candle or mild incense burning
- Have calming music playing softly as students arrive.

Spend some time practicing the techniques used in this lesson so you will be able to explain them from personal experience.

Notes:

Explanations of each are in the Bible Study Guide handout.

They are:
1. Guided Meditation (Opening Activity)
2. Lectio Divina
3. Ignatian Method
4. Creative Response

Pray for peace for yourself. Pray for a calm meeting. Pray for each of your students.

 # Leader Insights

Connecting to Your Students
Just as we need to prepare the resources for a lesson, we need to prepare our hearts and minds for the Biblical and theological insights each lesson provides. Familiarize yourself with these insights to help you respond to the discussion questions and activities throughout the lesson.

Explaining the Bible
The six styles of biblical criticism used by scholars are:
1. Textual criticism tries to reconstruct the original wording of the text.
2. Historical criticism tries to establish the time and place of writing, the circumstances behind the writing, the author, and the original intended readers.
3. Literary criticism examines vocabulary, syntax, and inflection. The idea is that the message of a book is revealed not just by what it says but also by how it is written.
4. Form criticism usually assumes that the supposed writer of the text was really more of an editor who compiled things from different sources and put them together in one work, and so focuses on the subdivisions within the text.
5. Redaction criticism makes that same assumption and focuses on how the whole work was edited together. (Neither form nor redaction criticism accuse the attributed writers of plagiarizing or lying.)
6. Canonical criticism asks questions such as: Why was this book placed where it is in the Bible? How does it affect the book, written to stand alone, to now be part of a larger work?

In this lesson, we're going to discuss how to use the Bible for what it's worth. We talk about reading the Bible, or studying the Bible, or 'spending time in the word.' All those phrases mean basically the same thing: trying to use the Bible to help us live better lives.

The way some Christians use the Bible is to ask God a question, then flip open the Bible, point to a random verse, and read it thinking that God will use that verse to answer their question.

Some people start with a topic or a question and then go digging for scriptures that speak to that topic or question. Sometimes that might work, and sometimes it might not. The Bible was not designed to be a search engine to find a quick and easy answer to every question in life. Some people read the Bible straight through from Genesis to Revelation just as they'd read a novel. This is a really impressive thing to do, but it's so hard to do that most people don't finish. Instead of starting with what <u>we</u> need or want, though, a much better way to use the Bible is to start with the scripture itself and see what <u>God</u> wants us to get out if it. Think of reading the Bible as a conversation with God.

The Bible was not written with 21st century North Americans in mind. It's a good idea to have some idea of who wrote the part of the Bible you're reading, for whom it was written, and the circumstances under which it was written. For example, when Paul talks about being in chains for Christ in Philippians, he really was chained up in prison! A quick and easy way to know these things is to check a good study Bible which has an introduction to each book of the Bible.

People who study the Bible professionally usually do so in a particular way. We don't have to do it just like them, but it may be helpful to know how the pros do it. There are six ways professionals explore the Bible. Each way is called a style of criticism, but that doesn't mean that their primary task is to find fault with the scriptures.

All these styles of criticism are really just academic exercise—fine for brainy professors in university offices—but not terribly practical for ordinary folks just trying to read the Bible. It's usually best for us to use an eclectic style of biblical criticism, drawing the useful elements from all these styles and ignoring the elements that don't help us hear what the Holy Spirit is saying to us through scripture.

Meditation Leader Tip

When leading the guided meditation, speak in a calm voice. Speak just loudly enough to be heard with a little effort. Speak in a rhythm: four or five words then a brief pause to inhale. Inhale through your nose, exhale through your mouth. It is a good idea to practice this with someone well before the meeting to perfect a calm, steady tone and rhythm. If anyone becomes disruptive, another adult should calm them or, if need be, escort them out of the room as quietly as possible. You should not break your role as guide.

Notes:

Maybe the most important thing in reading your Bible is finding one you can understand. Basically, there are two kinds of translations: word-for-word and thought-for-thought. Each has its own strengths and weaknesses. Word-for-word translations try to change as little as possible from the original writings, which sometimes make for awkward sentence structure. Thought-for-thought translations try to translate the same idea a particular passage is conveying, but use contemporary words and sentence structure. Paraphrases are a whole other thing—they try to preserve the meaning of a passage while freely changing sentence structure and word usage to sound pleasing to the ears, to be easier to understand, and possibly to appeal to a specific group of readers. 'The Hip Hop Bible' would be an example of a paraphrase.

Just like there are different types of TV shows, the Bible has different kinds of writing. So if we're going to try to read the Bible for maximum effectiveness, it's important to choose what part of the Bible to read. If you like stories, then try the Gospels. If you like poetry, then choose a Psalm. If you like history, then try 1 Kings. If you like action, then check out the story of Samson in Judges. If you like romance, then try Ruth or Song of Solomon. There are all kinds of different types of writings to read. You may want to start at the beginning of a book and read through it over time, or you may want to use a guide of some sort; many study Bibles include reading plans. For someone who has absolutely no idea where to start, the Gospel of Mark is a good place to start. It tells the story of Jesus concisely, much like a news account.

Reading the Bible is not like reading any other book. We read other books to gain information, to be entertained, or because we have to for school. We read the Bible to hear God. That's a big difference. If we're trying to hear something or someone, we need to be quiet. Reading the Bible should be done in a quiet place. That doesn't mean just a lack of noise, but a peaceful place with as few distractions as possible.

Most scripture when written was meant to be read aloud. Think about it: the stories passed down, the sermons of the prophets, the songs and poems--even Paul's letters were written with the expectation that they would be read aloud to a church's congregation. Always read scripture aloud, even if you're alone. The more senses you use--hearing and sight, instead of just sight—the more engaged in the text you'll be.

That's the goal of effective Bible reading: to be fully engaged. For that reason, don't just read, but immerse yourself in the scripture. After you find your quiet place, get your mind and heart quiet. Pray, asking God to speak to you through the scripture, and then read the scripture out loud. Remember, the goal of reading scripture is not to get through it, but to get into it! Don't rush. Read short passages. Go for quality rather than quantity.

Theological Underpinnings

The Cumberland Presbyterian Confession of Faith refers to the Bible as "the infallible rule of faith and practice," and affirms that God speaks through it. To hear and understand God, though, takes more than just reading scripture. We have to be open to the Holy Spirit, who transforms words written by people into the word of God (1.05-1.07). Reading the Bible (properly, at least) is unlike reading any other book. We don't do it for information or entertainment, or to feel better, or to pass a test, but to truly hear God. Through the work of the Holy Spirit, the Bible can be the means by which God transforms persons' lives. It is a resource that is never worn out or depleted, because the Spirit makes it ever fresh and always appropriate for the situation at hand, but we have to listen for God in the words of scripture.

Apply the Lesson to Your Own Life

What do you hear in "the infallible rule of faith and practice": that the Bible itself is infallible and inerrant, or that we can't go wrong when we follow the Bible's leading? What's the difference between these two ideas?

Why do you read the Bible most often: preparing to teach, for personal growth, to gain information, to prove someone else wrong? Do you usually go to the Bible to affirm something you already believe, or to seek some new insight? When do you get the most from scripture: when you're reading it by yourself, or when you're studying it with a group? Why do you think that is?

Think of the teacher or preacher in your life who most vividly made the Bible come to life. How can you do for others what that person did for you?

Most Christians would agree that although it is to be held in reverence, the Bible itself is never to be worshiped. Do you know anyone who borders on worshipping the Bible? Is it

Field Trip

There are many translations and paraphrases available today. Most church-going students have at least one Bible of their own, but it may have been a well meant but not well thought out gift rather than one they chose for themselves. Sometimes Bibles aimed at a particular audience such as "The Hunter's Bible" are nothing more than a marketing tool. Take the time to become familiar with several different translations and be ready to help students select an appropriate Bible. A great outing would be taking your students (individually or as a group) to a bookstore to spend some time comparing Bibles and purchasing just the right one. Shop online if you need to or gather good editions from folks in your congregation that students can explore. Prayer, discernment, exploration, and maybe even some trial and error is the best way.

Notes:

possible to make the Bible and idol? A weapon?

The Lesson

Get Started (10 min.)

Psalm 23 Guided Meditation

With everyone seated and still, turn off the music or reduce the volume until it's almost inaudible. To lead this guided meditation, use the speaking and breathing technique in the Meditation Leader Tip. Then follow the script below using these punctuation cues: a period or comma means a one-breath pause; an ellipsis means a ten to 20 second pause.

- *Everybody get still and quiet.*
- *Sit comfortably. Close your eyes.*
- *Take a few deep breaths. Inhale through your nose. Exhale through your mouth. Keep breathing like this.* (Just breathe for thirty to sixty seconds.)
- *Focus your heart and mind on God. Focus on hearing God. God's word to you right now.*
- *"The Lord is my shepherd."*
- *A shepherd leads. A shepherd guides. A shepherd protects the sheep.*
- *Remember the times God has led you, guided you, and protected you. Remember and be thankful...*
- *"I have everything I need."*
- *God provides all that we need. Even things we don't know we need.*
- *Remember a time God provided something you needed...*
- *"He lets me rest in green pastures. He leads me to calm water."*
- *Picture yourself in a peaceful place. The most peaceful place you can imagine...*
- *Feel your anxieties and concerns melt away. Feel the peace of God embrace you...*
- *"He gives me new strength."*
- *Imagine a task that you have to do. Feel God empowering you, to overcome the obstacles in your path...*
- *"He leads me on paths that are right for the good of his name."*
- *Envision a tough choice you're facing. Imagine it as a fork*

- *in the road...*
- *Look and listen for signs. Signs from God, showing you the right path to take...*
- *Commit to following those signs, stepping out in faith, even when the entire way is unclear...*
- *Promise God that you will trust God every step of the journey...*
- *"Even if I walk through a very dark valley, I will not be afraid, because you are with me. Your rod and your staff comfort me."*
- *Imagine something you fear. Picture it as a shadow. Now see it running away from the light of Christ...*
- *"You prepare a meal for me in front of my enemies."*
- *Envision a huge banquet table. There's food on the table. Lots of good food. It represents all the blessings God has given...*
- *"You pour oil on my head; you fill my cup to overflowing."*
- *Feel the Holy Spirit pouring over you. Feel God wrapping a robe around you...*
- *Envision the thing that makes you unique. The gift that God has given you alone, what God wants to give the world through you...*
- *"Surely your goodness and love will be with me all my life, and I will live in the house of the Lord forever."*
- *Imagine yourself years from now. You're grown, maybe married, maybe with kids...*
- *You're looking back on your life. What are you most pleased about?*
- *What have you allowed God to do for you?*
- *What have you allowed God to do for the world through you?... (Pause twice as long at this point. Then pray something like the following prayer, easing the rhythmic speech pattern a bit, but keeping your tone calm.)*
- *Thank you, Lord, for this wonderful Psalm and the promises it brings. Help us to hold on to those promises as we seek to hear and do what you want for our lives. Continue to speak to us, and to guide us. Speak to us always, Lord, and give us the faith to listen to you.*
- *(Remain silent for 30 to 60 seconds, and then end the prayer as you normally do or simply say AMEN.)*

Return to your normal speech patterns. If you need to increase the lighting in the room or turn off the music, do so slowly as you progress through the lesson.

Notes:

Just in Case:

Apocryphal Books

Some of your students may be interested in the Apocryphal books that Roman Catholics include as scripture and we do not. In 1548, at the Council of Trent, the Roman Catholic Church affirmed some extra books as scripture. Since this was after the Reformation had begun, the Protestant church didn't adopt these extra books.

Other writings exist which some say should be in the Bible. These are sometimes called "lost" or "secret" books, or perhaps the Gnostic gospels. Most of them were written well after the canonized books and have dubious authenticity.

Listen Up (15-20 min.)

Interactive Reading

Say: *Today we're going to use our time together to talk about how to use the Bible for what it's worth. We talk about reading the Bible, or studying the Bible, or 'spending time in the word.' All those phrases mean basically the same thing: trying to use the Bible to help us live better lives. What we just did is called a guided meditation, and its one form of Bible study.*

Discussion Question:
- What was your experience during the guided meditation?

Say: *The way some Christians use the Bible is to ask God a question, then flip open the Bible, point to a random verse, and read it thinking that God will use that verse to answer their question.*

- Do you think that is an effective method?

If time allows take a few questions from students and let them try the "flip and point" method for some good laughs.

Say: *Instead of starting with what we need or want, though, a much better way to use the Bible is to start with the scripture itself and see what God wants us to get out if it. Think of reading the Bible as a conversation with God. When you read, take time to stop and think and listen, like we did in the guided meditation.*

Discussion Questions:
- How do you watch a movie?
- How many of you sit back and let yourself be drawn in to the story?
- How many of you watch for mistakes?
- How many of you pay attention to how the scenes are edited together? Why?

There are lots of different ways to watch a movie, and there are lots of different ways to read the Bible. People who study the Bible professionally usually do so in a particular way. We don't have to do it just like them, but it may be helpful to *know how the pros do it. There are six ways professionals explore the Bible. Each way is called a style of criticism, but that doesn't mean that their primary task is to find fault with the scriptures.*

All these styles of criticism are really just academic exercise—fine for brainy professors in university offices—but not terribly practical for ordinary folks just trying to read the Bible. It's usually best for us to use an eclectic style of biblical criticism, drawing the useful elements from all these styles and ignoring the elements that don't help us hear what the Holy Spirit is saying to us through scripture.

Discussion Question:
- What kind of TV shows do you like best: documentary, medical drama, vampire drama, news, sports, situation comedy, soap opera, "reality," etc.?

Just like there are different types of TV shows, the Bible has different kids of writing. So if we're going to try to read the Bible for maximum effectiveness, it's important to choose what part of the Bible to read.
- *If you like stories, then try the Gospels.*
- *If you like poetry, then choose a Psalm.*
- *If you like history, then try 1 Kings.*
- *If you like action, then check out the story of Samson in Judges.*
- *If you like romance, then try Ruth or Song of Solomon.*

Reading the Bible is not like reading any other book. We read other books to gain information, to be entertained, or because we have to for school. We read the Bible to hear God.

Most scripture when written was meant to be read aloud. Think about it: the stories passed down, the sermons of the prophets, the songs and poems--even Paul's letters were written with the expectation that they would be read aloud to a church's congregation. Always read scripture aloud, even if you're alone. The more senses you use--hearing and sight, instead of just sight—the more engaged in the text you'll be.

The goal of effective Bible reading is to be fully engaged. For that reason, don't just read, but immerse yourself in the scripture.

Notes:

Notes:

 # Now What? (20-25 min.)

Application: 'Deep Reading'

Explain: *There are three simple ways to read the Bible deeply—to read it in a way where you interact with what you're reading. I'm going to explain these three ways and then we'll have some time for you to try one of them out.*

*The first way to read is called '**lectio divina**' which is a Latin phrase that means 'divine reading.' In Lectio Divina, you start by reading the text slowly with your full attention. Watch for some word or phrase to jump out at you. It may take a couple of readings for this to happen. Next, meditate on that particular word or phrase by concentrating on it fully. Then, pray the text back to God. You are, after all, trying to communicate with God, so rework the text into a prayer or just offer it to God as is. Finally, relax and listen. Instead of doing something with the text, allow the text to do something with you. When the time feels right, ask God to reveal how you can live out what you've heard in the text.*

*The next way of reading scripture is called the **Ignatian Method**, named after Ignatius of Loyola (1492-1556). This method works best with a passage that tells a story. As you read the text, imagine yourself in the story. Hear the voices and sounds, see the images, feel the ground under your feet, smell the fire or the food, feel the excitement or panic or fear in the story. You might be a bystander who sees everything that happens, or you might be one of the main characters (even Jesus). Using this method, you might use the same text several days in a row, changing which character you imagine yourself to be. Prayers using this method should focus on God revealing new things to you, especially by perceiving things from the perspective of Jesus.*

*The third way of reading scripture is the **Creative Method**. The creative method is spending time in a text and then creating some form of artwork. By using the creative portions of our brains, we can often find things in the text that our reasoning brains would miss. The artwork can be a poem, a picture (either a picture that looks like something real, maybe something from the story, or some kind of design, or a person's name written in an artistic way), a song, a sculpture, a* *dance, a percussion rhythm, a journal entry, a chord of music, or just about anything else you can create.*

After explaining the different ways of deep reading, give each student the "John 7:53-8:11" and "Bible Study Guide" handouts.

Ask the students to choose one of the ways of reading scripture that you've talked about and read this passage using that method. Point out the art supplies for those who wish to create something. Tell them they have 10 minutes, and then have them spread out as much as possible for privacy. Gently give a two-minute warning at the appropriate time, and then call the group back together after ten minutes.

Open the floor for anyone to share what they experienced, wrote, drew, or heard. Affirm that incomplete results are fine to share. This is a great opportunity to actively encourage all students to take the floor.

Live It (5 min.)

If your pastor publishes sermon texts or the youth leader announces lesson texts in advance, suggest to students that using these methods and spending time with those verses throughout the week before coming to church might be a good way to get started. That way, when they walk into church, they're prepared to get even more out of the worship service.

Close the lesson in prayer or ask a student to lead the group in prayer.

©2011 Discipleship Ministry Team of the Ministry Council of the Cumberland Presbyterian Church, All Rights Reserved.

Notes:

Bible Study Guide

📖 Choose a Bible you can understand.

📖 Have a plan by choosing what to read before you settle down.

📖 Expect not just to read the Bible, but to have a conversation with God.

📖 Find a quiet place free of distractions. Calm your mind and spirit.

📖 Read out loud, even if it's in a whisper.

📖 Choose how to read:

> *Lectio Divina* is four steps:
> 1) Read the text slowly with your full attention, watching for some word or phrase to draw your attention more than the others.
> 2) Meditate on that word or phrase by concentrating on it fully.
> 3) Pray the text back to God by re-forming the text into a prayer or just offer it to God as is.
> 4) Relax and listen. When the time feels right, ask God to reveal how you can live out what you've heard in the text.
>
> *Ignatian method* is reading the text carefully and injecting yourself into the story as an observer or one of the characters. What do you see, hear, taste, smell, and feel? How do you respond to what happens? Listen for something new God wants to tell you.
>
> *Creative method* means you create something after reading the text, letting it fill your spirit, and listening for God: a poem, a picture, a journal entry, anything.

📖 Give thanks to God for what God has revealed to you, even if it's just affirming what you already believed.

📖 Share and discuss with someone what you heard God say through the scripture.

📖 Commit to doing what you heard God say do.

📖 In addition to reading the Bible alone, also arrange to read it together with others (friends or family). Reading and reflecting with a group often leads to new insights.

John 7:53-8:11

Pharisees test Jesus

They each went to their own homes, and Jesus went to the Mount of Olives. Early in the morning he returned to the temple. All the people gathered around him, and he sat down and taught them. The legal experts and Pharisees brought a woman caught in adultery. Placing her in the center of the group, they said to Jesus, "Teacher, this woman was caught in the act of committing adultery. In the Law, Moses commanded us to stone women like this. What do you say?" They said this to test him, because they wanted a reason to bring an accusation against him. Jesus bent down and wrote on the ground with his finger. They continued to question him, so he stood up and replied, "Whoever hasn't sinned should throw the first stone." Bending down again, he wrote on the ground. Those who heard him went away, one by one, beginning with the elders. Finally, only Jesus and the woman were left in the middle of the crowd. Jesus stood up and said to her, "Woman, where are they? Is there no one to condemn you?" She said, "No one, sir." Jesus said, "Neither do I condemn you. Go, and from now on, don't sin anymore."

David and Goliath: Too Gory for a Kids' Story
By Andy McClung

Scripture: 1 Samuel 17:1-54

Theme: There's more to this story than the little guy beating the big guy; that can move students beyond a childish understanding of it to have God-given confidence in facing problems of their

Resource List

- Video Option 1: YouTube "Carolina Camera: The Sling Shot Man."
- Video Option 2: YouTube "Ancient Secrets of the Bible—David & Goliath" and "Lost Science of the Bible—Is the Bible's Account of David and Goliath Accurate?"
- Video Option 3: Clip from "The Empire Strikes Back" see Leader Prep for details
- A set of plastic armor and weapons or print out a drawing of Goliath that shows all the arms and armor mentioned in the passage.
- A small smooth stone for each student.

Leader Prep

- Locate the video options in the resource list.
- For Video Option 3: Clip from "The Empire Strikes Back" which shows Luke Skywalker first meeting Yoda while setting up camp after crash landing on the swampy planet Dagobah. The key clip is Luke saying, "I'm looking for a great warrior" and Yoda replying, "Great warrior? Wars not make one great," but you can use more of the film to frame this. The scene is at approximately 47:00 to 50:00, depending on the edition of the DVD. It's also available on YouTube under the title "Luke Meets Yoda."
- Print six to eight sheets of paper with quotes about war. Have a balance of pro, con, and neutral. Samples (feel free to just use these):

- "All war is deception." Sun Tzu
- "I have never advocated war except as a means of peace." Ulysses S. Grant
- "If we don't end war, war will end us." H. G. Wells
- "It is well that war is so terrible. [If not] We should grow too fond of it." Robert E. Lee
- "Never think that war, no matter how necessary, nor how justified, is not a crime." Ernest Hemingway
- "The scenes on this field would have cured anybody of war." William Tecumseh Sherman
- "There was never a good war, or a bad peace." Benjamin Franklin
- "War is an ugly thing, but not the ugliest of things. The decayed and degraded state of moral and patriotic

Notes:

feeling which thinks that nothing is worth war is much worse." John Stuart Mill
- "We are going to have peace even if we have to fight for it." Dwight D. Eisenhower
- "We shall defend [England], whatever the cost may be, we shall fight on the beaches, we shall fight on the landing grounds, we shall fight in the fields and in the streets, we shall fight in the hills; we shall never surrender." Winston Churchill
- "The only thing necessary for the triumph of evil is for good men to do nothing." Edmund Burke
- "We make war that we may live in peace." Aristotle

- If possible, put a piece of tape or a sticky note on the wall of your meeting space 10 feet above the floor. If your ceiling is too low, mark out ten feet horizontally on the floor or wall. To be extra creative, use chalk to draw a ten foot tall stick figure or outline of a man on the sidewalk or parking lot where your students will see it before entering the building, or use masking tape to make a similar figure on the floor of your meeting space.
- There will be a lot of scripture to be read during this lesson, so use an easily understandable version of scripture, such as *The Message* or the *New Living Translation*. Not familiar with the different translations? You can compare several different versions at biblegateway.com to make your choice.
- Pray for your students and yourself as you prepare to lead this lesson.

 ## Leader Insights

Connecting to Your Students

Just as we need to prepare the resources for a lesson, we need to prepare our hearts and minds for the Biblical and theological insights each lesson provides. Familiarize yourself with these insights to help you respond to the discussion questions and activities throughout the lesson.

This story is often familiar even to people who didn't grow up reading the Bible or going to Sunday school. In the secular world we hear this story alluded to—incorrectly--whenever a smaller entity goes up against a larger entity in politics, business, sports, or whatever. Newscasters talking about a new, small company taking on a large, well-entrenched company will make a reference to David and Goliath. The phrase has also been used to compare two sports teams: Goliath is the favored team and David is the underdog. One company even used a cartoon image of David clobbering Goliath to promote their training program: "How to Beat Goliath: A Practical Guide for Competing with Superstores." Such comparisons are incorrect because the story of David and Goliath is about far more than just a little guy taking down a big guy.

Explaining the Bible
Truthfully, we don't know how big Goliath was. Some translations offer a size description of "six cubits and a span." Scholars commonly agree that a cubit was 18 inches (the length of a grown man's arm from elbow to fingers) and a span was nine inches (the width of a grown man's hand with fingers spread). The Bible tells us that Goliath was well armed and well armored.

Goliath isn't the only 'giant' mentioned in the Bible. It tells us Goliath was from Gath. In 2 Samuel 21:15-22 mention is made of four other Philistine soldiers big enough to wield a spear the same size as Goliath's. In 2 Samuel 21:20 yet another supersized bad guy is mentioned, this one actually is said to be as big as a giant. Plus, he had six fingers on each hand and six toes on each foot! Theories are plentiful, but no one knows for sure why these Gath guys would have been so big. It may have something to do with their having in common an oversized ancestor, perhaps King Og of Bashan whose bed was 13½ feet long, and six feet wide (see Deuteronomy 3:11).

Scripture doesn't say, but David's father, brothers, and King Saul probably considered him too young to be trained as a warrior, which is why he was running food and messages back and forth instead of being there full time with Saul's army. Goliath calls him a kid. Combine this with the knowledge that in Jewish culture boys become men on their thirteenth birthday (adolescence is a fairly recent, and very western, concept) and we can safely say that David could have been 12 years old. If Goliath and the others were exaggerating to make a point (the equivalent of calling somebody a baby), it still stands to reason that David could not have been more than 15 to 17.

If the events of First Samuel are recorded chronologically, then David has already been secretly anointed as the new king of

Notes:

Leader Note:

His helmet would deflect arrows and swords, but apparently it didn't have much of a faceguard. His coat of mail was like a long shirt made of small interlocking rings of metal. It would keep arrows, swords, or anything else from piercing his arms, chest, belly, and thighs. Greaves are like the shin guards a baseball catcher or a soccer player wears. They would have protected his knees, shins, and the tops of his feet.

A javelin is made for throwing. Most of its power comes from gravity: you throw it in an arc and the force of gravity combines with the weight of the javelin to bring it down hard enough to pierce shields and armor. A spear, contrary to popular belief, is made for stabbing rather than throwing. It's long enough that the user could stab at an enemy while staying out of reach of the enemy's sword. The back end of the spear could also be braced against the ground when the enemy charged, which might make them impale themselves on it. And, of course, when the fighting got too close for anything else, Goliath would have dropped his spear, drawn his sword, and taken his shield from his shield bearer.

Israel by the priest Samuel (see 16:1-13) and God has removed any blessing from Saul. David knows he's God's chosen person to lead and serve the Israelites, but Saul is still officially the king. The events may not be arranged chronologically, however, for David and Saul get to know each other in Chapter 16, but then in Chapter 17 it's as if they've never met before. That's just a difficulty in this text we have to deal with. Difficulties such as this actually affirm the Bible's development and authenticity. If it was all just made up, then awkward bits like this would have been fixed to be more palatable.

Saul had displeased God by turning his back on God and not following God's commandments. God didn't want him to be king anymore (15:10-11) and had chosen David to replace him.

As the official king, it was Saul's job to defeat the Philistines, but he couldn't do it. Saul couldn't please God as king, so God chose David to be king; Saul couldn't get rid of the Philistines, so God chose David to do it.

All this doesn't mean, however, that David was any less arrogant. The scene in Saul's tent really shows us that David did not respect Saul as king (17:31ff). When David goes into Saul's tent he speaks first, which one was never supposed to do in the presence of the king; one was to wait until the king spoke to them. Saul tried to dismiss David, but even though the king's word is always supposed to be obeyed, David stood his ground and refused to be dismissed. So, yes, David was clearly arrogant. But he was also doing what he knew God wanted him to do.

After Saul agreed to let David fight Goliath, Saul stuck to what he knew and tried to outfit David in Saul's armor. But it didn't fit. It was too bulky, too heavy. David could barely move while wearing it. Surely the king's personal armor was the best armor to be had, but it was worthless—even detrimental—to David. What's best for one person may or may not be best for the next person. What's best for one person might actually be harmful to the next person. If David had faced Goliath wearing Saul's armor, he wouldn't have lasted a minute.

David's refusing to use Saul's armor also serves as a metaphor to show that David, as the new (though still secret) king, is not going to do things as Saul did them. Warfare as Saul knew it (and Goliath as well) is not David's way at this point in his life. He's going to do things his own way, putting his faith in God.

Theological Underpinnings
Trust is hard for some people. Trusting in God is no different. That's why people like David are heroes of the faith: they do things like step into the ring with giants! One might say that trust is faith in action (or even faith out loud). You might have *faith* that God will take care of you, but quitting your job and starting a mission in Africa takes *trust*.

In this lesson, the worlds of David and Goliath are explored and contrasted. Goliath lives to conquer, and trusts only the technology of his day. David lives to glorify God, and trusts the eternal God above all. David's trust is based partially on what God has done in the past, but he also has to have faith that God will continue to help him take down intimidating opponents. This lesson affirms that youth can do amazing things, despite what some adults tell them, but emphasizes that what really matters is what they do for God. Taking home a stone helps students carry the lesson with them into their daily lives.

Apply the Lesson to Your Own Life
There's an old saying: pray like everything depends on God, and work like everything depends on you. Do you believe that's valid? Do you live that way? To which side are you more likely to err: trying to do everything yourself, or expecting God to do everything?

This story seems to promote doing things in new ways. Are you comfortable with that? Do you try new things? Does your church? How do you determine where the line is between trying something new just to be trying something new, and trying something new because the old way isn't working well anymore?
Recall a time you really had to exercise trust in God. How does that compare with David facing a giant? Was your trust a conscious choice or your last resort? The next time you have to face a giant, remember little David and what God accomplished through him.

Notes:

Notes:

The Lesson

 # Get Started (8 min.)

Word Association Game

After your students get settled, explain that you'll be playing a word association game. You will say a word and they, all at once, are immediately to call out the very first word that pops into their minds. Say something like, "For example, if I were to say, 'Dog,' what's the first word that pops into your head?" Emphasize that the answer needs to be given immediately, with no thinking, deciding, or filtering.

When everyone is ready, run through four or five easy words (such as bunny, school, milk, pizza). Pause between words only long enough for everyone to answer. If needed, stress again that the answers need to come immediately. Keep going at the same pace, but move on to four or five slightly more involved words (such as algebra, dating, car, bully, litter). Keep going at the same pace and conclude with the word "war."

If you were able to hear some of the final responses, ask specific students to repeat theirs. If not, go around the group and ask random students to repeat their responses. Use these responses to dig a little deeper by saying something like, "*That's an interesting response. What do we think of war?*" Just listen. Don't agree or disagree with any opinions shared, but an occasional "interesting" or "say a little more" might be needed. This discussion doesn't need to go on very long, nor should it become a debate. The purpose is to get your students thinking about war.

Interrupt someone by standing and reading the war quotes you prepared. Don't comment, reply to questions, or allow discussion. Just read a quote and stick it to the wall somewhere in your meeting space, then read the next quote and stick it to the wall. Continue until you are out of quotes. The desired effect is for your students to be surrounded—emotionally and physically—by these words about war.

Close this activity by showing the clip from The Empire Strikes Back. Possibly repeat Yoda's words: "Wars not make one great."

Discussion Question:
- How do we hear about the story of David and Goliath in the world? In sports?

Say: In this lesson we're going to explore the story of David and Goliath, a story some of us have known since we were little kids. But how well do we really know it?

Listen Up (25-30 min.)

Goliath
Have someone read aloud 1 Samuel 17:1-11.

Point out where you marked off ten feet to indicate about how tall Goliath was.

If you have the toy armor, bring it out piece by piece as you teach or if you're using the drawing, point to the pieces as you mention them. See the Leader Note page for information about each piece.

In the ancient world, military conflicts sometimes were settled by champions rather than entire armies. Each general or king would choose one champion, the two champions would fight to the death, and the survivor's army would be the victor.

Discussion Questions:
- Why do you think they did it like this?
- Is it a good idea or a bad idea?
- Could warfare work like that today? Why or why not?

Say: Nobody knows what Goliath actually looked like. It's a good bet, though, that covered with armor, holding all those weapons, the combined estimated weight of the armor and weapons being 125 lbs. (more than most sixth or seventh graders), and standing taller than anybody else around he was a frightening sight. Worse, he was completely confident that he could kill any Israelite who dared to stand up to him.

David
Have someone read aloud 1 Samuel 17:12-25.

Discussion Question:
- How old do you think David was when this happened?

Notes:

Notes:

Leader Tip:
This story teaches us that throughout life other people will be telling us what is the best (the best phone, the best clothes, the best shoes, the best computer, the best kind of person to date, the best college, the best way to do something). But God made each of us differently. Our needs are different. Our personalities are different. Our strengths and weaknesses are different.

Say: *Today, rebel armies in some countries kidnap boys as young as eight or 10, kill their families, and then force the boys to fight other rebels or the government army. Often, the boys are forced to watch their families' murder, they undergo physical and emotional abuse, and they're desensitized to killing by being forced to kill. All of this makes them completely dependent on the rebels.*

Discussion Questions:
- How is this different from the U.S. drafting 18 year olds into the armed forces during both World Wars and Vietnam?
- Is 18 a reasonable age to be serving in the military?
- Should women be eligible for the draft too?
- Does anybody plan to go into military service after you graduate high school?

If you have any student with relatives who are serving, or have recently served, in a war zone, and if you think the student is reasonably comfortable doing so, ask him or her to share what it's like to have a loved one in a war zone. Draw attention to any of the quotes that are appropriate during this time of discussion.

Have someone read aloud 1 Samuel 17:26-39.

Discussion Questions:
- Is it possible to commit a completely unselfish act, a good deed for which you receive absolutely nothing in return?

- Why do you think David volunteered to stand up to Goliath?

Say: *That's a tough question to answer. At first glance it appears that he volunteers in order to stand up for God. After all, this loud-mouthed Philistine is out there day after day taunting God's people, calling them a bunch of chickens, challenging them to send somebody out to fight. David is loyal to God and to his nation, Israel, and confident of God's protection, so he volunteers to be the one to face the giant. On the other hand, though, as soon as David learns about Goliath he also hears the Israelite soldiers talking about the reward that will surely go to whoever kills the loudmouth. David's first question to the soldiers is about the reward that would be earned by killing Goliath. He waits until his second question to mention God.*

How David behaves in front of King Saul doesn't really make him look any better. When Saul says there's no way a kid like David can beat a warrior like Goliath, David starts bragging. He starts off by telling about all the wild and dangerous animals he's killed and then adds on a mention about God's protection. Of course, it may be that David knew what Saul needed to hear; a king in the middle of a war needed to hear about military-like victories before hearing that God is watching over David.

Discussion Questions:
- In volunteering to fight Goliath, is David seeking fame and glory for himself, or is he seeking to defend and honor God?
- Is he so full of himself that he thinks he can do what appears to be impossible, or is he supremely confident in God's protection?

It's a tough call. Either way, this story teaches us something important. If David was supremely confident in God, such behavior teaches us that when we are doing God's work we can accomplish what seems impossible. If David was just being arrogant, we are reminded that God can do amazing things through flawed and sinful people like us.

Discussion Question (optional):
- What's going on with David's brother, Eliab? Why's he so angry about David being there?

King Saul basically said David was too young to do this thing.

Discussion Question:
- Has someone ever told you that you're too young to do something you thought was important?
- How did you feel?
- What did you do? Looking back, do you think the person who said you were too young was right or wrong?

Explain: *After Saul agreed to let David fight Goliath, Saul stuck to what he knew and tried to outfit David in Saul's armor. But it didn't fit. It was too bulky, too heavy. David could barely move while wearing it. Surely the king's personal armor was the best armor to be had, but it was worthless—even detrimental—to David. What's best for one person may or may not be best for the next person. What's best for one person might actually be harmful for the next person. If David had faced Goliath wearing Saul's armor, he wouldn't have lasted a minute.*

Just in Case

Some students, for a variety of reasons, may believe war is a good thing under certain circumstances. Morals aside, some of the guys will likely think certain aspects of war are cool. As Cumberland Presbyterians, however, we consider war an "evil" on par with slavery. We neither condone war as a good thing, nor say it's never necessary. We believe that "God abhors all such acts which cause needless suffering and death" (*Confession of Faith* 7.06).

Notes:

David's refusing to use Saul's armor also serves as a metaphor to show that David, as the new (though still secret) king, is not going to do things as Saul did them. Warfare as Saul (and Goliath as well) is not David's way at this point in his life. He's going to do things his own way, putting his faith in God and using the gifts God gave him.

 # Now What? (10 min.)

There Will be Blood

Read: Have someone read aloud 1 Samuel 17:40-54.

Discussion Questions:
- Why do you think David picked up five stones?
- How could David have possibly won this fight?
- Could a kid with a sling really hit somebody in the head with enough force to kill?

Explain: *David was small and moving fast. Goliath was big and his weapons and armor were heavy: he would not have been the fastest guy around. Goliath may not have been trained or accustomed to hitting a small, quickly moving target with his javelin, and 17:48 does say David was running. A sling is a distance weapon. The only distance weapon Goliath had was a javelin: deadly if it hits, but once it's thrown, it's gone.*

Show one of the YouTube videos featuring the real sling. Note that when a sling is used properly it produces a small sonic boom, the same as when a whip cracks. That means the sling is moving at 761 miles per hour. The projectile, of course, isn't moving at the speed of sound... but it's still got to be moving awfully fast.

If time allows, show the YouTube video of the old man with the slingshot. Explain that while we often hear or say that David used a slingshot, people just use that term because it's familiar to us. The Bible is clear that David used a sling, not a slingshot.

Discussion Questions:
- Are there things people tell you that you are too small or too young to do?
- What is God calling you to do that others might think youth are too small or young for?

 ## Live It (5 min.)

Give each student one of the smooth stones and say, "Keep this rock somewhere, in your pocket, your purse, your school bag, your car, your bedside table. When it seems like the right thing to do, the thing God wants you to do, is impossible to accomplish, pull out this stone. Hold it and remember that God empowered David, about your age, to accomplish what seemed impossible. And believe that God can help you overcome what seems impossible."

Close the lesson in prayer.

Resources used in creating this lesson: *Confession of Faith of the Cumberland Presbyterian Church, First and Second Samuel: Interpretation Bible Commentary* by Walter Brueggemann

©2011 Discipleship Ministry Team of the Ministry Council of the Cumberland Presbyterian Church, All Rights Reserved.

Notes:

Good Kitty: Another Look at Daniel and Those Lions
By Andy McClung

Scripture: Daniel 6:1-28

Theme: Daniel's story is about more than God protecting him from those lions. It's about staying faithful in a culture that ignores, or even works against, God.

Resource List

- Three copies each of the Instant Skits "Short Sammy and the Bullies" and "Praying Pat Meets the Meanies"
- One copy of "Daniel Boot Camp" for each student
- Bibles

Leader Prep

- Room Set Up
- Decide which Getting Started activity you will use
- Check out the Simon Says You Tube video as suggested in the first Getting Started activity
- Pray for the class time, each of your students, and yourself as prepare to you lead this lesson

Leader Insights

Connecting to Your Students
Just as we need to prepare the resources for a lesson, we need to prepare our hearts and minds for the Biblical and theological insights each lesson provides. Familiarize yourself with these insights to help you respond to the discussion questions and activities throughout the lesson.

Explaining the Bible
Several years before the lions' den incident, the Babylonian king Nebuchadnezzar invaded Jerusalem, stole some sacred objects from the Jewish temple, and kidnapped four smart and well-educated Jewish boys. He planned to indoctrinate them into the Babylonian ways so he could exploit their intelligence. One of those boys was Daniel. For three years, Daniel and the other Hebrew boys refused to accept the Babylonian culture. (They ate a vegan diet!) At the end of their training and education, Daniel and the other Hebrew boys were ten times as smart as the local boys who'd received the same training.

Notes:

When Nebuchadnezzar had a weird dream, he wanted someone to tell him what it meant. He protected himself against phony wise men by insisting they first tell him what his dream was, and then interpret it. None of the local wise men were up to the challenge, but God told Daniel what the dream was and what it meant, and then Daniel told the king. The four Hebrew boys were promoted. The king had another dream. God told Daniel this second dream meant that Nebuchadnezzar would end up living like a wild animal until he acknowledged God, which is exactly what happened.

The next king Daniel served was Belshazzar, Nebuchadnezzar's son. Belshazzar, partying hard, violated the sacred objects his dad had stolen from the Jewish temple. Suddenly a hand appeared and wrote something on the wall. Who do you think was the only one who could read the writing? Daniel. He was promoted again, becoming the third most powerful person in the kingdom, which is pretty impressive for a foreign guy who was only there because he was kidnapped as a child.

When Belshazzar was killed, Darius became king. He put Daniel in charge of one-third of the kingdom and started making plans to make Daniel second-in-command. Others, who were jealous of the power Daniel was given, convinced Darius to pass a new law that said only Darius could be worshipped.

Even though Daniel had been kidnapped, taken from his home and family, forced to live in a foreign culture, and been taught all sorts of stuff he didn't believe, he'd never given up on God—the real God, not the made-up gods of the Babylonians. In fact, it was God who gave him the gifts to make it so high in the Babylonian government. Daniel still worshipped and prayed to God daily, which had just become illegal.

Darius was in bad spot. He really liked Daniel, but he'd made this law and Daniel had broken it, so Daniel was busted. Darius had to follow his own rules and have Daniel thrown to the lions. Darius felt really bad about it. He couldn't eat or sleep all night. Even though he didn't really know much about God, he hoped God would protect Daniel.

In the morning, the lions' den was opened and there was Daniel, without a scratch, giving credit to God for protecting him from the lions. Darius was so mad at the men who'd tricked him into putting Daniel in danger he had them thrown to the lions. Apparently, the lions were pretty hungry after not eating Daniel. They tore up the tricksters.

Darius was so impressed with God's protection of Daniel he made a law that everybody should respect God. So, by his faithfulness to God, Daniel influenced an entire kingdom.

Daniel trusted God even though he was surrounded by a foreign culture that was hostile toward everything he believed.

Theological Underpinnings

Most churched people know the story about Daniel being thrown into the lions' den and God protecting him. It's a good story that reminds us that God's got our backs, but when we look at Daniel's whole story we are reminded of so much more.

Toward the end of the Listen Up section, we will explore persecution and ask students to think about how they might use their gifts to influence others. Keep in mind that different persons have different personalities, different strengths, and different gifts. Some of your students might be good at boldly and directly speaking to others. Others might be better at calmly and persistently working around others' hesitations and defenses. A good comparison would be different coaches or teachers. One might say, "Look, dummy, here's how you do it. See? Now do it right." Another might take more time, leading the student to a certain point and then allowing the student to make the discovery for him or herself. Neither approach is inherently better or worse than the other, but different people typically do respond better to one or the other. The direct approach might work on someone for whom the calm approach would just bounce off of; the direct approach might scare away someone more open to a slow, calm approach.

Your students may express discomfort with the idea of influencing others. American youth culture is big on tolerance and not judging. If you detect this discomfort, even if it's not voiced, point out that we all try to influence others all the time. Who hasn't said at some point, "This movie is so good. You've got to see it," or "I'm not doing that, it's dumb"?

Applying the Lesson to your Own Life

What's your earliest memory of the Daniel and the lions story? When did you come to know there was more to his story than the lions' den? How has Daniel's story affected your life?

Media Option:

Bullying is the most common form of persecution presented in today's media. YouTube has several videos that you might consider using as your getting started activity. Or you might choose to create your own video or record the Instant Skits.

Notes:

Have you ever personally witnessed persecution, or the aftereffect of it? Have you ever personally experienced persecution? Answering that may be tough because persecution sometimes can be subtle or masked, making it hard to identify. Historically, when and where Christians have been persecuted, the Church grew significantly. Did your experience of persecution – or, do you think experiencing persecution would – strengthen your faith or damage it?

What is it that distracts your attention away from God? How can you become more focused, like Daniel?

Do you think the US is heading for all out persecution against Christians? If so, what will you do about it? If not, why do you think some believe so?

The Lesson

Get Started (8-12 min.)

Option 1: Simon Says
Play a game of Simon says. Your students probably haven't played Simon Says in years and they probably don't want to. But if you, as Simon, have the right skills it can be loads of fun. Go to YouTube and watch "Pernell Roberts playing Simon Says from BNS #12" to see how the best ever Simon, Lou Goldstein, does it. If you can be half the Simon he is your students will have fun.

Discussion Questions:
- What was it like having someone else telling you exactly what you can and can't do? In real life, when are the times you have to do what somebody else says?
- What are the consequences when you don't?

Explain: *We all have to endure some situations in which someone else is telling us what to do. That doesn't go away after we grow up. What's important for Christians is to discern when it's okay to do what we're told and when it's not okay"*

Option 2: Instant Skits (12 min)
Select six students—three each to perform the following two Instant Skits. The roles can be played by either gender. These

skits don't need any rehearsal. Just hand each actor a script; give them a minute to look it over and then say, "Action!" Be sure to encourage applause after each performance.

Instant Skit: Short Sammy and the Bullies
Actors needed: Bully 1, Bully 2, Short Sammy (If you have a student who is shorter than average, <u>do not</u> make him or her Short Sammy. Instead, make him or her one of the bullies and make the tallest student Short Sammy, but make him or her play the role while kneeling.)

Stage Direction: Put Short Sammy in the middle of the performance area and encourage all the actors to ham it up.

Instant Skit: Praying Pat Meets the Meanies
Actors needed: Meanie 1, Meanie 2, Praying Pat
Stage Direction: Put Praying Pat in the middle of the performance area and tell him or her to kneel and act as if praying.

Discussion Questions:
- What was the difference in what the bullies did to Short Sammy and what the meanies did to Praying Pat?
- What is persecution?
- Did one of these skits show persecution? If so, what was the other skit demonstrating? If not, what did it show?
- What's the difference between that and persecution?

Explain, if necessary: *The bullies were mean to someone based on something beyond the victim's control. The meanies were mean to someone based on a choice the victim had made. The meanies were actually engaging in persecution. Dictionary.com gives the definition of 'persecution' as 'to pursue with harassing or oppressive treatment, especially because of religion... or beliefs.'*

Say: This kind of persecution is extremely mild compared to what some Christians go through in order to practice their faith in some parts of the world.

Notes:

Notes:

 # Listen Up (25 min.)

Daniel and the Den

Have someone read aloud Daniel 6:1-9. Drawing on the background information, explain how Daniel and the other Hebrew boys ended up in the royal courts of Babylon, how Daniel ended up in a position of power there, and how he remained faithful to God.

Have someone read aloud Daniel 6:10-18. Briefly explain that Darius didn't want to hurt Daniel, but had to follow the rules.

Discussion Questions:
- Have you ever had to choose between following the rules and hurting somebody you liked?
- Which did you choose, the rules or your friend?
- What influenced you to make that choice?
- How did your choice make you feel?
- What did you, or will you, do the next time you're in such a situation?
- Looking back, can you see a way you could have avoided the situation all together?

Have someone read aloud Daniel 6:19-24. When the reading is done, say nothing for a moment. This is a powerful scene. Let it speak for itself.

Have someone read aloud Daniel 6:25-28.

Discussion Questions:
- Can passing a law make somebody believe something?
- Can a Christian force others to believe in God or to trust in Jesus? How or why not?
- What might be a better way to influence someone's beliefs and decisions?
- How do you influence others' decisions?

Say: *Daniel trusted God even though he was surrounded by a foreign culture that was hostile toward everything he believed.*

Discussion Questions:
- Is the culture we live in hostile toward our faith?

- When was the last time you saw a Christian portrayed in a movie, a TV show, a novel, a comic book/graphic novel, a commercial, or a song?
- Were they portrayed positively or negatively?
- Do you see positive or negative portrayals of Christians more frequently?
- Is that persecution?

Now What? (8-10 min.)

Is it Persecution?

Designate one side of the room as "Yes, It's persecution," and the opposite side of the room as "No way, not persecution." Read off the following situations and ask students to move to the side of the room they think fits the situation.

- *In June 2011, a university student in India was arrested and charged with evangelization and propagation of the Christian faith. A university professor was fired for the same reason. Is that persecution?*

- *In July 2011, Christians in Eritrea (a country in Eastern Africa) were being imprisoned for gathering to worship. Is that persecution?*

- *A few years ago in Indiana, a local doughnut shop (of a national chain) advertised that any school student who got an A also got a free doughnut, but then refused to give a student a doughnut for making an A in Bible class. Is that persecution?*

- *Dr. Caroline Crocker, a college biology professor, spoke of Intelligent Design in a class and pointed out some problems with the theory of evolution. She subsequently lost her job. Is that persecution?*

Have students to return to their seats and explain:
Persecution of Christians is a very real thing in our world. Some people believe it's only a matter of time before Christians are persecuted in the U.S. Others think it's already happening, but in subtle ways. Either way, the culture is much less friendly toward Christians than in recent generations.

Just In Case

Your students may zero in on verse twenty-four and ask why the tricksters' families were killed too. In that time and in that place, as was true in many ancient and even some contemporary cultures, the father represented the whole household. For good or bad, big things or small things, whatever the father did affected the whole family. If the father rescued a drowning princess, the king showered the whole family with gifts; if the father ran over the princess' foot with a wagon wheel, his whole family got thrown in jail for a few days.

Notes:

Notes:

Those of us in the church do need to be aware of such things happening around us. We don't need to blow things out of proportion to incite fear among believers, but neither do we need to let ourselves be bullied into silence by those who either don't know God or are antagonistic toward God. The more aware we are of obvious persecution happening around the world, the more easily we will be able to detect it at home.

 ## Live It (5 min.)

Explain: *Daniel lived in the middle of a lot of distractions, but by keeping his focus on God through prayer and worship, he was able to overcome the distractions and do amazing things for God.*

Prayer: *God, we pray that you give each of us the strength, the courage, the faith, and the wisdom that you gave to Daniel so that we can serve you better, whether we're in familiar surroundings or in places that seem like foreign lands. Amen.*

Resources used in creating this lesson: dictionary.com, persecution.org, The Washington Post article "Eden and Evolution" 2/05/2006

©2011 Discipleship Ministry Team of the Ministry Council of the Cumberland Presbyterian Church, All Rights Reserved.

☐DANIEL BOOT CAMP☐

The story of Daniel is about a whole lot more than God protecting some guy who got thrown in a lions' den. It's about how to live faithfully when the world around us ignores God… or even when the world around us is hostile toward God.

Over the next few weeks, go to "Daniel Boot Camp" and do each of these exercises. See if you notice a difference in your spiritual strength—how close you are to God.

☐ Pay close attention to how Christians are portrayed in movies, TV, books, and secular songs. Journal about how this makes you feel.

☐ Read the whole book of Daniel. It's not very long and it's full of interesting stuff. (Notice that it's not written in chronological order. Why do you think this is?)

☐ The name "Daniel" means "God is my judge." For the ancient Hebrews, a judge was not someone who decided guilt or innocence, but someone who decided what was God's will and what wasn't.

- ☐ What does your name mean?

- ☐ Who helps you decide what's God's will and what isn't?

☐ The "Daniel Diet" shows that what you eat really does matter (Chapter 1), but what matters even more is keeping yourself pure.

- ☐ Keep a journal for a week, recording absolutely everything you put into your body and mind – food, drink, reading materials, TV, movies, school work, music, magazines, websites. Try to write stuff down as soon as you do it so you don't forget.

- ☐ At the end of each day, record in a different journal when you felt closer to God and when you felt farther away from God that day.

- ☐ At the end of the week, compare your two journals and see if what you feed your body and mind is affecting your relationship with God.

☐ The story about the three guys being thrown into the fiery furnace, but not dying, in is the book of Daniel (Chapter 3).

- ☐ Tell someone the story of Daniel and these three guys. Ask them who they think the fourth person in the furnace was.

☐ The phrase "The writing on the wall" comes from this book of the Bible (Chapter 5).

- ☐ Listen for someone to use the phrase "the writing on the wall." When they do, ask them if they know where the phrase comes from. If they don't know it's from the Bible, tell them the story.

☐ In your prayers this week, ask for the strength to focus of God amid all distractions.

Instant Skit: Short Sammy & the Bullies

(Parenthesis give you actions to go with the lines being spoken.)

(**Bully 1** and **Bully 2** approach **Short Sammy**)

BULLY 1: Hey, Shorty! How's the weather down there?

BULLY 2: Looks like it's gonna be short with a chance of more short.

SHORT SAMMY: (Looks upset or sad)

BULLY 1: (laughing) Aww, don't get upset, Sammy. (Holds out hand at knee level) Gimme a LOW five.

BULLY 2: (laughing) Hey, watch out, Sammy. Don't trip over that worm!

BULLY 1: (high fives Bully 2) Good one! (Turns back to Sammy.) We're just kidding, Sammy. We really like you. In fact, I'd like to give you a few bucks.

BULLY 2: You're gonna give Sammy money? Why?

BULLY 1: 'Cause it looks like he's a little short!

(**Bully 1** and **Bully 2** walk away laughing.)

Instant Skit: Praying Pat Meets the Meanies

(Parenthesis give you actions to go with the lines being spoken.)

PRAYING PAT: (Kneel in the middle of the stage as if you're deeply in prayer. Don't look up, pray through the entire skit, ignoring the Meanies.)

(Meanie 1 and Meanie 2 approach Praying Pat)

MEANIE 1: Hey, Pat. Did you fall asleep or are you praying again?

MEANIE 2: Looks like praying to me. What an idiot!

MEANIE 1: Yeah. There's no God up there to hear your prayers. You'd be better off sleeping.

MEANIE 2: (laughing) Or hanging out with us.

MEANIE 1: Yeah, Pat. We've got whatever you could want. What's God ever given you?

MEANIE 2: (pushes Pat a little bit) I bet you've prayed for God to make us leave you alone, haven't you?

MEANIE 1: But here we still are! That's because your God doesn't exist, Pat.

MEANIE 2: Idiots like you made him up because they're just too weak to make it in the world.

(MEANIE 1 and MEANIE 2 walk away laughing.)

What's the Big Deal with the Big 10?
By Andy McClung

Scripture: Exodus 20:1-17

Theme: God gave the Ten Commandments to the Israelites not as a burden for them or to impose on others, but to teach them and set them apart from the rest of the world as a model for others.

Resource List

- Whiteboard or newsprint
- Markers
- Pad and pen for every four to six students
- One copy of "The Big 10" handout for each student

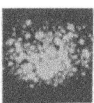

Leader Prep

- A space big enough for your whole group to gather and move around
- One sheet of newsprint with the Ten Commandments listed, preferably not numbered (keep this hidden until you need it for the lesson). You can either quote scripture directly or summarize and paraphrase.
- If you happen to have a poster or plaque of the Ten Commandments in your meeting space, remove it before the meeting.
- Pray for your students and yourself as you prepare to lead this lesson.

Leader Insights

Connecting to Your Students
Teens need rules, and they know it; but teens don't like rules, and they sure don't like admitting they need rules. Focusing on the Ten Commandments as a guide for living in a way that honors God, rather than presenting them a list of prohibitive rules, may sneak around your students' natural defenses.

Teens particularly dislike rules which seem to have no purpose other than to limit their freedom, so spending time on the reasons behind God's rules is s good idea.

Explaining the Bible
Through Moses, God had rescued the Israelites from slavery in Egypt. But they had been enslaved in a foreign land for so long

Notes:

Just in Case:

If the controversy over public display of the Ten Commandments has affected your town, and students bring it up, consider showing both sides of the issue, and where both sides agree. Some Christians seem to think that if everybody follows the Ten Commandments the world will be a better place, so they encourage everybody to do so. Other Christians believe that God only expects those who believe in God to follow the commandments so that we'll live differently from others and thereby model the best way (God's way) to live. This latter group may think it's pointless to force the Ten Commandments on others because people can't truly or fully follow them without having a relationship with God first. All Christians, however, agree that the Ten Commandments are a great map (or GPS, or directions from a helpful person) to help us find the best route through the journey of life.

they didn't know God very well. To reacquaint them with him, God decided to give them a set of rules to live by. This list opened with what we call the Ten Commandments, four of which deal with how the Israelites should treat God, and six of which deal with how they should treat each other.

The Bible itself never numbers the commandments. Any numbering is purely the work of humans and is therefore arbitrary. Considering Exodus 20:3-6 as one commandment makes the prohibition against idols refer only to God. In other words, no idol is to be made to represent God. Some Protestants criticize Roman Catholics for the statues of the saints they have in their places of worship, saying they're idols. But nobody worships those statues. Instead, they help Roman Catholics worship God. No icons representing God are used by Roman Catholics, in keeping with their understanding of Exodus 20:3-6. Different understanding, different traditions, same scriptures, same God, same reverence: there's no need to accuse fellow believers of idol worshiping.

Children don't get to know their parents just by following the household rules. But, by following the rules, children gain the opportunity to know their parents as more than just the rule-makers and enforcers. It's the same with us and God. We can't fully know God only by following the Ten Commandments, but by following them we become free from the things that keep us separated from God and, therefore, can come to know God more fully.

When God gave the commandment to have no other gods, other gods surrounded the Israelites. The Egyptians worshiped dozens of gods, and the different cultures the Israelites passed through in their wilderness journey had a bunch more. Following this commandment meant a radical departure from the ways of the rest of the ancient world. It also allowed the Israelites to show the world that God alone is worthy of human worship.

Few people today are tempted to worship ancient Egyptian gods (although that kind of stuff is still around, and may even be growing), but people do "worship" other things besides God. That means humans still are making our own gods today.

"You shall not make an idol" is closely related to the "no other gods" idea. In fact, some Christians consider 20:1-2, "I am the Lord your God," as the first commandment and 20:3-6 as the second commandment. (LI#2)

Of all of the commandments, this one may seem like the easiest to keep. But when it was given to the Israelites, this commandment was seriously counter-cultural. The Egyptians had idols to go along with their many gods. *Ra* was the sun god. His idol was a man with a bird's head. *Bast* was the goddess of protection. Her idol was a cat-woman or a large cat. *Sobek* was the crocodile god. His idol was… well… a crocodile. Maybe these specific gods were why God was so specific that no idols be made "in the form of anything that is in heaven above (Ra), or that is on the earth beneath (Bast), or that is in the water (Sobek).

We may look at idol-worshipers as pagan or simple-minded or even evil, but idol-making probably started out as more as an attempt to honor God. Early peoples knew that something greater than what they could see and touch was out there, so they fashioned physical objects to point them toward the spiritual: a bull represented strength, an eagle represented freedom, a gazelle represented swiftness and beauty. Maybe idols were a necessary step in humankind's attempt to figure out God. Where God drew the line, though, was when people began to see the idols themselves as worthy of worship. So, while we may not be tempted to bow down in front of a jewel-encrusted statue of some monkey god nowadays, we may still be in danger of treating some physical thing, even something that's supposed to point us toward God, as equal to or more important than God himself.

Different translations and paraphrases of scripture use different words. Some translations add clarity and some add confusion. The King James Version says, "Thou shalt not take the name of the Lord thy God in vain," which makes no sense to anybody younger than seventy-five. Eugene Peterson's *The Message* may put it best for today's youth: "No using the name of God, your God, in curses or silly banter."

In many ancient cultures, to know someone's name was to have a certain amount of power over that person. To say that person's name was to exert some of that power. Even though God loves us enough and wants to be in relationship with us enough to reveal his name to us, God does not want us using his name carelessly, such as saying things like, 'Oh. My. God. Did you see those shoes?' Nor does God want us using his name in a way that doesn't match his nature such as, 'No I don't have any spare change. Get a job you god d**n bum!'

Media Option:

You might lead into your discussion about the 10 commandments by using a funny video clip from YouTube like the Mel Brooks 10 Commandments clip.

Notes:

Leader Tip:
In Cumberland Presbyterian theology, we do make a choice to come into relationship with God through Jesus Christ, but it is God who calls us into that relationship and gives us the faith to respond. God chooses us first and then we respond (see Confession of Faith 4.02-4.03)

God was modeling for us the best way to live: working hard for a while and then taking a break to rest and rejuvenate. One might even consider God's actions on the seventh day as capping off creation by creating a renewing rest to better appreciate all the other work of creation.

The basic idea of taking a day off from work probably wasn't unheard of in the ancient world, but God first spoke this commandment to a bunch of recently freed slaves, so the idea may very well have been alien to them. The reason behind this commandment, however, was uncommon. God told the Israelites to take a day of rest every week, not just to relax and recharge, but to honor God. God knew then what we would later write in our Confession of Faith: 'The proper observance of the Lord's Day enriches the quality of life for all other days' (6.24). Regular and intentional rest and worship help us develop, maintain, and deepen our relationships with God.

We live in a culture that says if you're not busy, then you're not worthwhile. Because of this attitude we also live in a culture with burn-out, stress-induced heart disease, strained relationships within families, and lots of other problems caused by our constant busyness. God calls us Christians to combat the belief that says busyness equals worth.

How We Treat Others
The next commandment marks the shift from the commandments teaching how we should treat God to those teaching how we should treat each other. That shift, however, may not be as severe as it sounds. After all, how we treat others reflects what we believe about God, and what we believe about God affects how we treat others. The two actions are intricately and inseparably related.

The ability to share with God in creating new life is an amazing gift. Maybe that's why Martin Luther said God exalts parenthood as the highest human status. And maybe that's why the consequences of misusing that gift are so harmful. Likewise, God sees the family as very important because God knows it's in the home that we first learn what it's like to love and be loved, to have someone make sacrifices for us, to forgive and be forgiven, and to be dependent on someone else for life itself. This commandment is meant to strengthen the home and the family, whether it be a natural family or an adoptive or foster family.

Killing

There has been a lot of debate among Christians over the commandment which forbids killing. Did God mean all killing or just murder? What about self-defense? What about war? What about accidents? The Hebrew word used here can mean to intentionally murder a person, to kill someone by accident, or even to execute a convicted criminal. Only killing animals is not included in the meaning. What the word means exactly depends on the context it's used in. With this commandment, though, God offers no context. Perhaps that means God knows the best way for us to live is by taking care to never kill each other.

Some Christians extend the ban on killing to include any actions that take away or diminish life in any way, such as poverty, oppression, bigotry, etc. This may seem to be stretching things a bit, but does sound more sensible when we remember that Jesus said being angry with or insulting someone isn't that much different from taking a life (Mathew 5:21-26). Our Confession of Faith says that God abhors anything that causes needless suffering or death (7.06).

Killing is forbidden because God's original plan—the plan we humans messed up by sinning—was all about life. Genesis 1:28-31, 9:3-6, and Isaiah 11:6-9 give us an image of God's original plan. That image has no room for killing.

Adultery

People usually take this to mean 'Don't cheat on your spouse once you're married,' but Christians as far back as the 1200s have understood adultery to mean any sex outside of marriage.

It's no accident that the ban against adultery follows the ban on killing. Both are detrimental to society. Sex outside of marriage may be fun in the moment, but makes home—which should be the one place in the world everyone feels safe—an unsafe place (maybe not physically, but certainly emotionally). Because stable homes are the foundation for a stable society, this becomes a large scale problem very quickly.

God is concerned with both. And what we do with each has a great effect on the other. Christianity is not anti-sex as people seem to think. In Genesis 1:28 tells us to continue the work of creation by making more human beings. That only happens through sex. Most Christians believe sex is a good thing and are thankful God invented it. We also believe, and history has

---

Leader Tip:

Associating God with something from nature can limit our image of God to what we can understand about that natural thing. God wants to be known for who he is and not only for what he's done or made.

Notes:

Leader Tip:

"Covet" is a word that has little or no meaning to today's youth. "Lust" is a good substitute, but it's normally associated with sexual urges. Wrongful sexual desire is a part of this commandment's prohibition, but only a part. Maybe "inappropriate desire" is a good substitute for "covet."

proved, that this gift is best when used according to its inventor's instructions. (There is a entire Faith Out Loud lesson on sex.)

Stealing

Virtually every culture throughout history has agreed that stealing is wrong and bad for the society. The disagreement arises when we try to define stealing. Sure it's stealing to break into somebody's home and take a TV. But is it stealing for a starving man to break in and take some food for his family? Sure it's stealing to promise employees a certain wage and then deliver less than promised. But is it stealing for the boss to pay low wages so he can make more money himself? Most Americans wouldn't even consider stealing a bag of rice from a hungry village in an undeveloped country, but most Americans help waste enough food every year to feed the world. Is that stealing? Is it stealing to jack up the price of batteries during a blackout? Is it stealing to keep the extra money when a cashier gives you too much change?

Maybe the problem lies in us not knowing what's mine and what's ours, what stuff is for me alone, and what stuff is for everybody to use and enjoy. The answer to such questions, though, is really quite simple. Everything belongs to God. God is kind enough to allow us to use some of his stuff, and expects us to use it in a way that pleases him and helps others, especially the poor (Confession of Faith 6.10).

There will always be people who take, by force or deceit, what they have no right to. But one has to wonder: if we all did a better job of managing what God has entrusted to us, might there be less need for some people to steal? After all, this commandment is about God's concerns for people's needs. It's not really about material things or private ownership of stuff.

Lying

God created us to be in community. Lying about others damages that community. Proverbs 6:16-17, 25:18, Psalm 101:7, and other scriptures assure us that God hates lying in any form, so it's interesting that here in the commandments, God specified not to lie about other people. Lying is bad enough, but it's even worse when our lies harm other people. In short, bearing false witness against others is stealing and killing their reputation.

Among the commandments which speak to how we treat

each other, the one about coveting is the least concerned with actual behavior. It seems to be far more concerned with our thoughts and feelings, the actions of our hearts.

Most people would agree that killing, committing adultery, stealing, and lying are bad things, but we live in a world that actively promotes coveting through advertising.

With this commandment, God wants those who know him, those who follow him, to focus on him first and foremost. This is not because God is worried that we'll find something better and forget about him, but because God loves us enough to want us to keep focused on what truly matters. The things we covet, lust after, and drool over don't really matter in the long run. Only God does.

Theological Underpinnings

There is too much information here to cover in one gathering, so plan your class well. The lesson spends more time on the commandments that focus on how we treat God, and less time on those dealing with how we treat each other. This is to emphasize that when we focus our energies on living by the first group of commandments, the arguments and details of the second group become much less pressing. Be attentive to which commandments your students *need* to discuss (which is not necessarily the same as what they *want* to discuss) and spend more time on those topics. You might also consider breaking the study up into two weeks.

Applying the Lesson to Your Own Life

Do you think everyone should be expected to follow the commandments, or just believers?

What do you wish God had included in the Ten Commandments? Which of the commandments do you have the most trouble keeping? Who or what needs to be taken out of your life for you to do better in this area? Who or what needs to be added to your life for you to do better in this area?

Which of the commandments do you most often witness others breaking? Which commandment does it bother you most to witness someone breaking? Why that one?

Do you believe it's better for Christians to focus on following the Ten Commandments or Jesus' command to "love the Lord your God with all your heart, and with all your soul, and with all your mind, and with all your strength,' and to "love your

Notes:

Notes:

Leader Tip:
Point out those answers that have more to do with the fan than the team (I like their uniforms, they're from where I live, they're the best and I want to be associated with the best).

The Lesson

 ## Get Started (12 min.)

Forced Choice

Have your students gather in the middle of the room. Explain that you will give them two choices and they have to choose one or the other immediately. No indecision or third way is allowed. They make their choice by moving to the part of the room you point to. If they can't decide they should choose the answer that's most true for them. Do this a few times with easy choices. After everyone has chosen, ask a few from each side to share why they made that choice.

- *Would you rather step on dog poop or gum?*
- *Would you rather be too cold or too hot?*
- *Would you rather drink Coke or Pepsi?*
- *Would you rather water ski or snow ski?*
- *Would you rather stub your toe or bonk your head?*

- *Would you rather be rich or famous?*
- *Would you rather be valedictorian or voted most popular?*
- *Would you rather change a dirty diaper or unclog a toilet?*
- *Would you rather eat your favorite food every day for a year or once a year for the rest of your life?*
- *Would you rather star in a movie or direct a movie?*

Save time for these questions that introduce the study:
- *Would you rather tell someone what you believe about God or show them?*
- *Would you rather just start off on a road trip and trust your GPS to get you there or use a map and plan your trip?*
- *Would you rather stop and ask directions or keep trying to find it on your own?*
- *Would you rather keep playing this game, or sit down and start the lesson?*

Regardless of how students answer, it's time to start the study.

Listen Up (40 min.)

Name the Big 10

Start as a group by seeing if you can answer these questions:
- How many of the Ten Commandments can we name?
- Where have you seen the Ten Commandments listed?

Write down on whiteboard or newsprint any commandment named, even if what's said isn't really one of the Ten Commandments.

Now place your prepared list of the Ten Commandments side-by-side with the students' list and point out how well the class did in naming them. Congratulate them on however many they got right, and then (unless they aced it) point out that even though these commandments are easily available to us, maybe even around us a lot of the time, we still don't know them by heart.

Say: *We can't fully know God only by following the Ten Commandments, but by following them we become free from the things that keep us separated from God and, therefore, can come to know God more fully.*

The First 3

Have someone read aloud Exodus 20:1-3.

Discussion Question:
- Why do you think God was so uptight about the Israelites worshiping other gods?

Explain, if necessary, how God wants to be in relationship with his people. Other, false, gods, would interfere with that.

Discussion Questions:
- Who's your favorite team?
- Why are they your favorite? (Encourage answers beyond, "I dunno.")

Explain: *In the ancient world, people chose a god to worship in the same way as we choose our favorite teams. They'd move to a new place and start worshiping the same god as the*

Notes:

Leader Tip:
Some worldly ideas about the Ten Commandments that may have crept into your students' thinking: 1) people who follow the Ten Commandments perfectly can earn their way to heaven, or worse, 2) people who keep more commandments than they break are okay in God's eyes. Both ideas, of course, are false. As Cumberland Presbyterians we know salvation comes through God's grace: neither our faith nor our actions can earn it (see *Confession of Faith* 4.08-4.11).

Notes:

locals. They would worship the gods associated with their livelihoods. They'd choose the god who seemed more powerful than their enemies' gods. And all these gods were just made up by people to explain the supernatural.

Have someone read aloud Exodus 20:4-6.

Say: *"You shall not make an idol" is closely related to the "no other gods" idea.*

Discussion Questions:
- What are some things people treat as more important than God?
- What are some things we, the people in this room, treat as more important than God?

Say: *This may seem like the easiest commandment to keep, but really, we're surrounded by things that we can make into idols.*

Explain how the Israelites were surrounded by false gods and idols, especially the three Egyptian gods mentioned.

Discussion Question:
Our Confession of Faith says, "God is the creator of all that is known and unknown. All creation discloses God's glory, power, wisdom, beauty, goodness, and love" (1.10).
- So why would God not want us to use images from creation to represent him?

Explain how idol-making may have started out as an attempt to honor God.

Discussion Questions:
- Of all the things you have—actual physical items—which one would cause you the most spiritual distress—not emotional or financial—if it was lost or destroyed?
- Are you in danger of making that thing an idol?

Have someone read aloud Exodus 20:7.

Say: *Another way to say this is, "No using the name of God, your God, in curses or silly banter."*

Discussion Question:
- How many times a day do we hear someone say "Oh my God" or "I swear to God"? How many movies have "god d**n" in every other line of dialogue? Do these actions violate this commandment?
- Is it a violation of this commandment when someone commits murder in the name of God, like a terrorist or an abortion clinic bomber?
- What about when a president says it's God's will to declare war on another country?

Have someone read aloud Exodus 20:8-11.

Say: *This idea is reflected in our Confession of Faith: 'The proper observance of the Lord's Day enriches the quality of life for all other days' (6.24). Regular and intentional rest and worship help us develop, maintain, and deepen our relationships with God.*

Explain that the commandments already covered deal with how we should treat God and the rest of them deal with how we should treat each other.

Say: *That shift, however, may not be as severe as it sounds. After all, how we treat others reflects what we believe about God, and what we believe about God affects how we treat others. The two actions are intricately and inseparably related.*

How to Treat Each Other
Have someone read aloud Exodus 20:12.

Say: *God sees the family as very important because God knows it's in the home that we first learn about love, and sacrifice, and forgiveness, and depending on someone else for life itself. This commandment is meant to strengthen the home and the family, whether it be a natural family or an adoptive or foster family.*

Have someone read aloud Exodus 20:13.

Discussion Questions:
- Do you think God means this to be murder or all killing?
- What about war? Self-defense? Mercy killing? Hunting?
- Why do you think God ois so worried about people dying. Isn't death just part of life? Isn't everybody going

Notes:

Leader Tip:
Youth, especially, may see this commandment as unfair. What if your parents aren't worthy of honor? What if your parents aren't Christians? What Christians of all ages need to bear in mind is that this commandment is more than instructions for children. It also places a huge expectation on parents to live honorable lives. Parents who expect their children to follow this commandment must follow it themselves... and all the others too!

Notes:

to die sooner or later anyway?

Say: *Our Confession of Faith says that God abhors anything that causes needless suffering or death (7.06).*

Have someone read aloud Exodus 20:14.

Discussion Questions:
- What does adultery mean?
- What are the consequences when people break the commandment not to commit adultery?
- What are the consequences when people keep it?

Explain: *It's no accident that the ban against adultery follows the ban on killing. Both are detrimental to society. Sex outside of marriage makes home an emotionally unsafe place. Because stable homes are the foundation for a stable society, this becomes a large scale problem very quickly.*

Discussion Question:
- Why is God so concerned over what we do with our physical bodies? Shouldn't God be more concerned with our spiritual lives?
- Is Christianity against sex?

Explain, if necessary, how God invented sex and most Christians believe, *and history has proved, that this gift is best when used according to its inventor's instructions.*

Have someone read aloud Exodus 20:15.

Discussion Questions:
- Is it stealing for a man to take some food for his starving family?
- Is it stealing for the boss to pay low wages so he can make more money himself?
- Is it stealing to waste food?
- Is it stealing to jack up the price of batteries during a blackout?
- Is it stealing to keep the extra money when a cashier gives you extra change?

Explain: *Maybe the problem lies in us not knowing what's mine and what's ours, what stuff is for me alone, and what stuff is for everybody to use and enjoy. The answer to such questions, though, is really quite simple. It's all God's. God is kind enough to let us use some of his stuff, and expects us to use it in a way that pleases him and helps others, especially the poor (Confession of Faith 6.10).*

Discussion Question:
- If we all did a better job of managing what God has entrusted to us, might there be less need for some people to steal?

Have someone read aloud Exodus 20:16.

Discussion Questions:
- Do we break this commandment if we speak falsely about God?
- What are some lies people tell about God?
- What harm might these lies do?
- Other scriptures say God hates lying, so why do you think this commandment specifies lying about other people?

Have someone read aloud Exodus 20:17.

Explain: *Imagine a TV commercial for a plumber. 'Toilet backed up? Call Pete the Plumber!' Now imagine a TV commercial for the latest smart phone: long, caressing shots of the device, images of all the fun things you can do with it, maybe pictures of oh-so-happy people using it. These two things are advertised differently because one is needed and one is not. Wanting something that's not needed, especially when you want it because someone else has it, is coveting.*

Discussion Question:
- Do you think God included this commandment because he's afraid we'll find something better than him?

Now What? (10 min.)

How Many Thou Shalt Not's Make a Thou Shalt?

Give each group a pad and pen and instruct them to rewrite the Ten Commandments in positive and contemporary language. For example, instead of "don't commit adultery,"

Leader Tip:

If your group is large enough, break up into groups of four to six. If your group is small, just separate into two groups or even stick together.

Notes:

make it "keep sex within marriage".

Allow five or six minutes for this exercise, and then come back together and have someone from each breakout group share what they came up with. Discussion may follow, encouraged by questions from you such as: does your version send the same message as the original? Is this easier to understand? Would it be easier to tell a non-Christian friend about the Ten Commandments using this language?

Edit together one list of 10 using the best-written positive language commandments and brainstorm ways to share it with the congregation (bulletin, newsletter, posters, a creative presentation in worship).

Live It (5 min.)

Pass out copies of "The Big 10" handout

Say: *God gave us the Ten Commandments not to burden us with rules, or to control what we do, or to scare us into obedience, or to force them on others, but in order to teach us how to live in a way that puts us in right relationships with God and one another. When we who seek to know God live by these commandments, this gift from God, we are able to build trusting relationships with both God and one another and thus help create a better world.*

Prayer: *Thank you, God for your gift to us of the Ten Commandments. Help us to live by them so that we, and those whose lives our lives affect, may truly live the best way possible. Amen.*

Resources used in creating this lesson: <u>The Truth About God</u> by Hauerwas and Willimon, <u>Smoke on the Mountain</u> by Joy Davidman, and dictionary.com.

©2011 Discipleship Ministry Team of the Ministry Council of the Cumberland Presbyterian Church, All Rights Reserved.

THE BIG 10

The Ten Commandments

1. No other gods besides God
2. No idols
3. Use God's name respectfully
4. Take time to relax and focus on God (keeping the Sabbath)
5. Honor your parents
6. Don't kill anybody
7. No sex outside of marriage
8. No stealing
9. Don't tell lies about people
10. Don't drool over what other people have

Did you know...

... the Bible never numbers the Ten Commandments, or even calls then "the Ten Commandments"?

... the Ten Commandments are in the Bible twice? Check them out in Exodus 20:1-17 and in Deuteronomy 5:6-21.

... that images of Moses and the Ten Commandments are all over Washington D.C.?

... the first Christians were raised Jewish so for awhile they doubled up and lived by both Jewish and Christian standards. This meant resting from work on the Sabbath (Saturday) and then worshiping God through Christ on Sunday (because Jesus was resurrected on Sunday.)

Things to think about and act on this week:

- Which commandment do you have the most trouble keeping? Is there something in your life (a relationship, a behavior, a temptation, etc.) that you can change or add to your life to better follow this commandment?

- Challenge your entire household to take off one whole day. No homework, no practice, no chores, no going to work. Use this time – together and alone – to pray, relax, study scripture, do good deeds for others, and sit quietly in God's presence. Sit down as a family later on and talk about the experience.

- Remember a time someone lied about you, by either spreading rumors or intentionally trying to hurt you. Have you forgiven that person? If not, pray for strength to do so. Then commit to only speaking the truth about others.

The next time you really want something, stop and ask yourself: Do I want it because someone else has it, or do I really need it? Did I decide I want it, or did someone else somehow tell me I want it?

Is "Judgment House" Evangelism?
By Andy McClung

Scripture: Isaiah 41:10

Theme: To help students consider—rationally rather than emotionally—fear-based evangelism efforts, and to offer them a broader view of evangelism.

Resource List

- Video Clip: "A Letter from Hell" from YouTube or GodTube. There are several versions of this video; choose one that you think will work best with your group. If it helps, the audio element of this "letter" is more important than the video element.
- Ten to 12 images cut from magazines, or printed from the web (See Leader Prep for details)
- Index cards or construction paper with fears written on them (See Leader Prep for details)
- Pens and paper.
- One copy per student of the handout "Is Judgment House Evangelism?"

Leader Prep

- Room Set Up
- Find 10-12 images to use with the "Images" activity. Suggestions: a fancy car, an attractive girl, a attractive guy, a very diverse group of people, a sports team in action, a small child but not an infant, a path in the forest or a park with no people visible, an old person, two empty chairs facing each other, a disaster scene, a family at the dinner table, an authority figure (teacher, coach, police, etc.). It'd be great if some of the images are black and white. If your church owns *Every Picture Tells a Story* (Zondervan / Youth Specialties, 2002), you can use its pictures.
- If you're not familiar with the concept of Judgment House, spend some time on the Web watching video clips of them. Pay attention to comments left by other viewers. At judgmenthouse.org this event is defined as "a dramatic walk-through presentation about the truth of people's choices and their consequences both in this life and the next. No other tool is more effective at presenting people with an opportunity to choose a personal and saving relationship with Jesus Christ." Basically, though, Judgment House is a dramatic play in which the audience walks through the scenes and watches different characters make good and bad choices in life, then the characters die tragically, and then the audience sees some characters go to heaven and others go to hell. Producing and hosting these events require great expense of time, effort, and money. The churches that do so consider it evangelism.
- Write different fears on cardstock or construction paper, making one for each student. Examples: fear of water, fear of fire, fear of dogs, fear of snakes, fear of spiders, fear of

Notes:

heights, fear of being in a tiny space, fear of flying, fear of speaking in public, fear of death, fear of the dark, fear of going to the dentist, fear of getting a shot, fear of storms. Make them common fears, not some clinical rarity. Keep these cards concealed until time to use them.
- Pray for wisdom as you lead and for the Holy Spirit to open the hearts and minds of your students during this lesson.

 ## Leader Insights

Connecting with Your Students

In this lesson, we are talking about fears. It is important to keep in mind that youth are not yet fully in control of their emotions or their thoughts: both their brains and their psyches are still developing. They may believe themselves to be grown up, they may try to act grown up, they may demand that they be treated as grownups, but they're not grownups.

Also note that teens enjoy being scared while knowing they're really safe (scary movies, haunted houses, roller coasters). Judgment House plays to this. You can too. As Isaih says, we can be in fear-producing situations while knowing that we really are safe in God's hands.

Explaining the Lesson

Fear is an emotion, and some emotions are good (love, contentment, happiness, joy, affection, feeling proud of your accomplishments). Sometimes thinking can overcome emotions, but more often, it seems, strong emotions can overcome a person's ability to think. Contemporary language does a poor job of distinguishing between feeling and thinking. We say, "I feel it would be best for all involved if we did it this way," when we really mean "I think this is the best way to do it."

Thinking is not fully devoid of emotion, of course, but problems arise when emotions override thinking. Don't believe this? Consider a horny teenage boy who has just received an invitation to have sexual intercourse with a teenage girl. He knows that sex before marriage is wrong. He knows that unprotected sex can lead to pregnancy and disease. He knows he may get into big trouble with his parents, her parents, or both. But in that moment his thinking is in grave danger of being overridden by his emotion.

Likewise, relying solely on logic and reason does not make a healthy person. We've all known someone who caused awkward situations by stating facts and logic without consulting his or her emotions first. A well-adjusted individual will have found a balance between the two. Keep the balance of these two in mind throughout this lesson.

God gave us fear to keep us safe. We're *supposed* to be a little afraid of dangerous places and animals so that we'll be careful around them. But fear is just an emotion. Fear itself can't hurt us. What happens more often is that we hurt ourselves—physically, emotionally, or even spiritually—because our fear of something is out of proportion to the threat that thing actually poses to us.

Anexample of disproportionate fear causing as much or more damage than the actual threat would be a guy who is so completely afraid of heart disease that he worries about everything he eats and drinks, and freaks out when he can't get to the gym. He worries about avoiding heart disease so much, in fact, that he has a stress-induced heart attack.

Evangelism may be a scary word to some youth (it certainly is to many adults), but, basically, evangelism is simply telling someone else about something good you've found. Rather than telling someone about a good movie, or book, or website, though, you're telling them about something that really matters: Jesus.

Many Christians claim that they don't have the gift of evangelism. So what? Those who are particularly gifted at evangelism may end up doing it as a vocation, but all Christians are called to share the good news of Jesus. And each person has his or her own way of doing that best.

Some people are fine with the **confrontational style**. Persons with this style are confident and direct in their approach. They skip small talk and get right to the point. Such an approach might not work in every situation, however, which is why God gives us each different personalities.

Some people are better with the **intellectual style** of sharing their faith. They use reason and logic to express their faith and try to get others to join them. These persons might like to ask leading questions to open up a conversation to the topic of faith.

Others are better simply at sharing what God has done for

Leader Tip:

An example of disproportion between fear and threat your students may be familiar with is the "stranger danger" program. Having secret passwords with trusted adults, don't talk to strangers, don't print your child's name on lunch boxes or school bags—these are elements of the stranger danger education. The idea is to help keep children from being the victims of abductions. The disproportion, however, comes from the fact that only a tiny percentage of child abductions are perpetrated by a complete stranger. It's usually a trusted adult who does the abducting.

them. This is the **testimonial style**. These people are good listeners, good storytellers, and good at drawing connections between their own lives and the lives of those to whom they are speaking.

Those who are outgoing, love a good conversation, focus on other people and their needs might be good at the **interpersonal style**. They build friendships with the persons who they want to tell about Jesus.

People who are hospitable, persuasive, and loyal to the things they're involved in are good at the **invitational style**. They enjoy meeting new people and inviting them to church activities.

The **serving style** is one which has been pushed in youth ministry circles for years, maybe even to the detriment of nurturing these other styles. Those who use this style of evangelism prefer to show their love by actions more than by words. They enjoy doing good things for others. They're good at noticing needs and meeting those needs, and they don't mind doing work for others that is dirty or menial. Persons who are good at this style express the love of Christ by showing love for those in need.

Theological Underpinnings

In the Bible, almost every time a human has a close encounter with a supernatural being (angel, resurrected Jesus), that being says something along the lines of "Fear not." Fear is a very real life experience, but – other than the awed respect the Bible translates as "fear of the Lord" – God doesn't want us to be afraid of what God is doing for us.

Throughout the New Testament, however, there is evidence that God *does* want us to tell people about Jesus. Telling people what Jesus has done for us, how he loves everyone, how he only wants the best for us, how he died so that we can live life abundantly… that's called evangelism.

Bullies and terrorists have to keep making new threats, and occasionally actually hurt someone, to keep their victims in fear. To continue motivating someone by fear, you have to keep them afraid. Persons who accept Christ only because they fear dying tragically and going to hell will soon find that fear wearing off and, with it, the motivation to change their lives. Using fear to motivate someone to make a decision for Christ just doesn't make sense in the long run. Do we use fear to convince someone to watch a movie or to read a book we enjoyed? No, we tell them how good it is, how much we enjoyed it, and we let them know we want them to have that same pleasure.

Apply the Lesson to Your Own Life
How clearly do you distinguish between thinking and feeling? How well do you balance them?

Write a journal entry about what you think about evangelism, then write how you feel about it. Watch the news from a purely rational perspective and determine how many of the stories play upon viewer's fears. Recall someone you've met who used fear in trying to convert people to Christianity. Did it work? Did those conversions last?

If you've ever been to a Judgment House, recall your emotions there, then think about the whole experience (was fear involved, the blatant message of the storyline, the underlying messages of the storyline, how guests were treated afterwards, how the invitation to talk with someone was made). Are your emotions and your thoughts in agreement as to the experience's value?

Aside from the incredibly important task of teaching teens, how do you practice evangelism?

The Lesson

Get Started (10 min.)

Option 1: Fear Factor

Have students, one at a time, stand in front of the others. You sit behind the standing student and hold up one of the cardstock signs you've made. The standing student must ask questions which the others may answer only with "yes" or "no" to determine what his or her pretend fear is of. If you wish to have a winner, it'd be the person who guesses correctly with using the fewest questions. If you have a particularly large group, you may want to divide into two groups for this game, or simply have only some of your

Notes:

Notes:

front of the group. You, behind her, randomly select a card and show it to the group. It says, "Fear of Dogs."
Sarah: Am I afraid of some kind of place?
Group: No.
Sarah: Some kind of animal?
Group: Yes.
Sarah: Is it spiders?
Group: No.
Sarah: Snakes?
Group: No.
Sarah: Is this animal usually bigger than spiders and snakes?
Group: Yes.
Sarah: Am I afraid of dogs?
Group: Yes!
Leader: Good job, Sarah, you got it with six questions. Who's next?

Option 2: Fearful Charades

Using the fear cards, play a game of charades. Allow each student a chance to silently act out the fear listed on his or her card while the rest of the group tries to guess it. If you wish to have a winner, it'd be the person who gets the group to guess correctly in the shortest time. Do not force shy students to perform in front of the others, but do give them the chance to choose for themselves to do so.

 # Listen Up (25 min)

Opening Question:
- What are you really afraid of?

As students answer, ask for a show of hands from those who share the stated fear.

Say: *God gave us fear to keep us safe. We're <u>supposed</u> to be a little afraid of dangerous places and animals so that we'll be careful around them. But fear is just an emotion. Fear itself can't hurt us. What happens more often is that we hurt ourselves—physically, emotionally, or even spiritually—because our fear of something is out of proportion to the threat that thing actually poses to us.*

Images

Divide your students into two groups. Tell one group they are the thinkers. They are to turn off their emotions and respond to this activity with pure rationality. Tell the other group they are the feelers. They are to turn off all logic and respond to this activity with pure emotion.

As an example, show the picture of the fancy car. Say: *When I look at this car I **feel** speed, being popular, having fun, I'd love to have it. When I look at this car I **think**, the color is the same as my dog's eyes, it's got to be expensive, the insurance must be ridiculous, it gets poor gas mileage, would a bike rack look good on it?*

One by one, reveal the images you have prepared. Display the first and give instructions to study the image in silence. After about thirty seconds, ask how the image made the feelers feel. After responses, ask what the thinkers think about the image. Go through as many of the images as seems productive and alternate which group responds first. Listen for anyone saying they are in the wrong group and praise them for knowing themselves well enough to recognize that, but also affirm that everyone needs to develop both parts of ourselves: feeling and thinking. When you've run out of images or time, ask the following questions. Or incorporate them into the discussion as you go.

Discussion Questions:
- How hard was it to ignore one part of you and focus fully on the other?
- Which are you more comfortable with, your thoughts or your feelings?

Letter from Hell

Show the "Letter from Hell" video and/or play the audio.

Discussion Questions:
- How did that make you feel?
- What do you think about this letter?

Explain, in a non-biased way, what Judgment House is and that the churches which produce these plays do so as evangelism.

Discussion Questions:
- What is evangelism?
- Have any of you been to a Judgment House, or a youth

Notes:

Leader Tip:

If your students need help, ask some questions to stimulate their thinking and reduce their emotional response. How could a letter be written in real time, while this guy is being dragged off to hell? How could a letter survive the flames? How could this letter have been delivered to earth from hell?

Notes:

rally where the speaker said things such as, "You could die in a car crash on your way home tonight?" What are they trying to accomplish?
- Have you ever seen a guy on the street corner waving a Bible and shouting such things as "Turn to Jesus now, before it's too late!" What does he mean?

If someone has had such an experience, ask him or her to share about it. If they don't offer it in their narrative, directly ask how they *felt* during the event, and then what they *thought* during the event. How do they feel about the event now?

Activity: Scripts

Explain that you're going to summarize some stories. The students' job is to decide which story is from a real Judgment House script, used by churches to share the love of Christ with the people in their town or city. Read all of the summaries and then have students vote which story they think is the one really used in a church's judgment house. The stories:

- *A non-churched family accepts an invitation to attend a church. The teenage daughter accepts Christ there, but no one else in the family does. The family returns home and are all murdered in a home invasion. The daughter goes to heaven and the rest of her family goes to hell.*
- *Two middle school cheerleaders are abducted by two men they don't know. The adult with them is stabbed to death during the abduction. While the girls are held captive, they talk about God. In the end, one of the girls is killed and the other survives.*
- *A teenage boy reluctantly attends church camp. He doesn't feel accepted anywhere, including among the church kids. The only person that makes him feel loved is his grandmother. While at camp he gets a message that she has died. This, added to his rejection by the church kids, is too much. He kills himself.*

Tally up the votes to see which script your students think is the real one, then announce that these are <u>all</u> real scripts written to be used by churches in Judgment House events. (They can be found at judgementhouse.org.)

Discussion Question:
- What do most of these scripts have in common?

Explain, if necessary: *The main idea these stories have in common is fear. Fear is a great motivator. Fear can make people accomplish amazing things. The problem is that fear is only a good motivator for a little while.*

Discussion Questions:
- Has someone ever convinced you to do something by using fear? Would you tell us about it?
- Have you ever convinced someone to do something by instilling fear?
- Can anybody remember a story from the Bible in which Jesus used fear to get someone to follow him?
- What's a better way to convince someone to try something you know is good?"

As you go through the following explanation of different ways one can be an evangelist, ask at the end of each type for a show of hands of who identifies with that way of sharing Jesus.

Say: *Evangelism may be a scary word, but, basically, evangelism is simply telling someone else about something good you've found. Rather than telling someone about a good movie, or book, or website, though, you're telling them about something that really matters: Jesus.*

Many Christians claim that they don't have the gift of evangelism. So what? Those who are particularly gifted at evangelism may end up doing it as a vocation, but all Christians are called to share the good news of Jesus. And each person has his or her own way of doing that best.

6 Styles of Evangelism
*Some people are fine with the **confrontational style**. They're confident and direct in their approach. They skip small talk and get right to the point.*

*Some people are better with the **intellectual style** of sharing their faith. They use reason and logic to express their faith and try to get others to join them. They might ask leading questions to open up a conversation to the topic of faith.*

*Others are better simply at sharing what God has done for them. This is the **testimonial style**. These people are good*

Just in Case

Fear of the Lord?

You may have a student who knows scripture well enough to ask something like, "If God doesn't want us to be afraid, then what about all that 'fear of the Lord' stuff in the Bible?" While God does not want us to live in fear, because we are human beings—tiny, sinful, and insignificant compared to God—human beings can't help but be a little bit afraid when in the presence of God. Until we have been resurrected, that is. A better way to say "fear the Lord" may be "have an awed respect for God."

Notes:

confident and direct in their approach. They skip small talk and get right to the point.

Some people are better with the **intellectual style** of sharing their faith. They use reason and logic to express their faith and try to get others to join them. They might ask leading questions to open up a conversation to the topic of faith.

Others are better simply at sharing what God has done for them. This is the **testimonial style**. These people are good listeners, good storytellers, and good at drawing connections between their own lives and the lives of those to whom they're speaking.

Those who are outgoing, love a good conversation, focus on other people and their needs might be good at the **interpersonal style**. They build friendships with the persons who they want to tell about Jesus.

People who are hospitable, persuasive, and loyal to the things they're involved in are good at the **invitational style**. They enjoy meeting new people and inviting them to church activities.

The **serving style** is good for those who prefer to show their love by actions more than by words. They enjoy doing good things for others. They're good at noticing needs and meeting those needs, and they don't mind doing work for others that is dirty or menial. Persons who are good at this style express the love of Christ by showing love for those in need.

 # Now What? (5 min.)

Will I share?

Give students a piece of paper and a pen. Encourage them to write down the names of five friends or acquaintances with whom they would like to share Christ. Encourage them to pray over the list and ask God to give them opportunities to share God's love the way they know how to best.

Live It (5 min.)

Pass out copies of "Is Judgment House Evangelism?"

Say: *Some people who do not know Jesus need that in-your-face kind of evangelism. Some people need a good scare to make them pay attention. Nothing else will reach them. It does indeed work sometimes. But most of the time it seems to either turn people off or only get a quick emotional response rather than a deep, heart-felt, life-changing response. No matter how a person makes a decision for Christ, though, the church's job (and therefore all Christians' job) is to nurture them and help them grow in faith.*

Prayer: *Thank you, God, for making all of us different. Thank you for calling and equipping those of us who have entrusted our lives to Jesus to share the good news about the salvation he offers. May we do it well, in a way that makes lasting disciples. Amen.*

Resources used in creating this lesson: judgementhouse.org, *Becoming a Contagious Christian* by Bill Hybels

©2011 Discipleship Ministry Team of the Ministry Council of the Cumberland Presbyterian Church, All Rights Reserved.

Notes:

Is "Judgment House" Evangelism?

Feeling vs. Thinking - Finding a Balance

Be aware of how you respond to everything, whether it's with your feelings or with your thinking. Ask God to help you know when to trust your feelings, when to trust your thoughts, and when to

Don't be Afraid

Did you know the Bible is full of God or God's messengers telling people, "Don't be afraid"? God does not want us to turn to him in fear, but to respond to the love he has shown us through Jesus.

Here are some of the places you can find God telling people not to be afraid:
Genesis 15:1, Genesis 26:24, Exodus 14:13, Deuteronomy 1:21, Joshua 1:9, Psalm 56:11, Isaiah 41:10, Isaiah 43:5, Jeremiah 42:11, Matthew 1:20, Matthew 28:5, Luke 1:13, Luke 2:10, John 14:27, Acts 18:9, Revelation 1:17.

What's your style?

Telling people about Jesus is no different than telling them about a movie or book you like… except that Jesus is way more important. Different people have different styles of telling people about Jesus. Which one fits you best?

▶ **Confrontational:** You like to use the direct approach. See Peter in Acts 2 for an example.

▶ **Intellectual:** You use logic and reason. See Paul in Acts 17 for an example.

▶ **Testimonial:** You share your own story about what God has done for you and through you. See John 9 for an example.

▶ **Interpersonal:** You establish a friendship before sharing Jesus. See Matthew in Luke 5 for an example.

▶ **Invitational:** You invite others to church events and introduce them to others who will tell them more about Jesus. See the woman in John 4 for an example.

▶ **Serving:** You show God's love by seeing needs and meeting them. See Dorcas in Acts 9 for an example.

Notes:

Worship: BOOMM or GROOL?
By Andy McClung

Scripture: Psalm 86:8-10

Theme: Students may view worship as boring and pointless. This lesson teaches why we do what we do in worship and clarifies that our worship is primarily about pleasing God, not us.

Resource List

- A video camera (recommended, but optional)
- Marker
- Whiteboard or newsprint
- Praise music and player
- Several copies of typical Sunday bulletins (not necessarily the same day) or a print out of the typical order of worship from your church
- One copy of BOOMM or GROOL? Handout for each student

Leader Prep

- Arrange space appropriate for performing a skit. (Nothing fancy, just enough space to move around a bit and allow for both performers and an audience.)
- Consider having worship music playing softly as students arrive, or maybe even throughout the entire meeting. "Heart of Worship," "You Are My All in All" and similar songs would be good for this.
- If you advertise upcoming studies, you may need to explain to adults that BOOMM is "bored out of my mind" and GROOL is "great + cool." If these text abbreviations are no longer in use, or not well known in your area, substitute similar ones that are.
- Pray for wisdom and guidance as you lead this lesson, that the Holy Spirit be at work in the hearts and minds of your students, and that God be pleased with what comes of this lesson.

Leader Insights

Connecting to your Students
Just as we need to prepare the resources for a lesson, we need to prepare our hearts and minds for the Biblical and theological insights each lesson provides. Familiarize yourself with these insights to help you respond to the discussion questions and activities throughout the lesson.

Notes:

Youth often see worship as dry and boring. In some cases they are right, but anyone can benefit from better understanding why we do what we do in worship. This lesson will give them a chance to offer feedback on the weekly worship experience in your church. More importsntly, it will equip them with the vocabulary to make that feedback informed and constructive.

Explaining the Lesson

Based on the guidance of our CPC Confession of Faith 5.12 the most appropriate Christian worship is to be worshiping a triune God (Father, Son, Spirit) through Jesus, the Christ, rather than worshiping Jesus alone.

In this lesson, we will cover elements of worship which the Cumberland Presbyterian Directory of Worship (bound with the *Confession of Faith*) suggests for inclusion in every worship service. Because every church is different, though, each of these elements may not be included in your typical service. Likewise, your service may have elements not reflected in these notes. If your services have elements not included in these notes, then ask whoever designs the services to provide you with a brief theological explanation of those elements to share with your students. Note: baptism and Holy Communion are not covered in this lesson because each of these sacraments has an entire lesson dedicated to it within this series.

This lesson is arranged a bit differently from the others in this series. Rather than offer background information in this section, it is incorporated into the Listen Up section, below. This should help you keep from having to flip pages as you teach.

Theological Underpinnings

The most important thing about worship to keep in mind, and the most important thing to instill in your students, is that worship is all about God... not us. Worship services should be designed not to please the worshippers, but to please God. The soloist's song, the choir's singing, the money we drop in the offering plate, what we wear, how we act—none of it is done to please any human being in that room, but to please God.

There is nothing in the Confession of Faith about church attire, but there are almost certainly unwritten expectations about it within your congregation. How people, especially youth, dress for worship can be a hot topic at many churches.

If there are certain adults in your church who openly gripe about the youth group's casual attire, take a moment during the "I'd Dress Up for That" activity to explain to your students that dressing up for church is very important to such persons.. It offends them to see others not doing what they think is the only right way to be. Don't take sides, just ask your students to try and see things from the complainers' perspective.

Hopefully, the activity will make the point that we dress up for important events.

Apply the Lesson to Your Own Life
Try to recall a worship service that almost bored you to death. What made it so bad? Was it something the worship leaders did or didn't do, or did it have more to do with your attitude that day? Try to recall a worship service that you couldn't get enough of. What made it so compelling? Was it something the worship leaders did or didn't do, or did it have more to do with your attitude that day?

Do you pay equal attention to every element of the worship service? If not, which element do you pay more attention to?

Do the worship planners and leaders seem to pay equal attention to every element of the worship service?

Does it help you worship to say and do the same things week after week (doxology, Lord's Prayer, etc.), or does this allow you to worship on automatic pilot?

Do you believe that worship is about God, not us? Does your worship reflect how you answered that question?

Notes:

Notes:

The Lesson

Get Started (15 min)

Silent Skits

Divide students into two groups. (If you have a particularly small group do both skits as one group, but do them in sequence.) Explain that each group will have five minutes to prepare a silent skit—no sounds, no noises, no talking—on a topic that you will give them. Separate the two groups, placing them in separate rooms if at all possible.

Assign one group the topic "a typical worship service at our church." Do not show them a bulletin or order of worship, as part of the exercise is seeing which elements of the service they can remember and which they find forgettable.

Assign the other group the topic "the groolest worship service ever."

After each group has had five minutes to prepare, call them back together.

Have the "typical worship service" group go first. If you wish, record the skit with a video camera. Encourage wild applause from the audience. Next, have the "groolest worship service ever" group make its presentation.

Have each group offer feedback and questions to the other. You may need to guide them with specific questions or observations (what was going on when..., why did everybody look so bored when..., why was everybody so excited when..., do you think their skit was a good representation of a typical worship service here, do you think their skit would really be a good worship service).

Spend some time discussing what you noticed in the skits, especially elements of worship the youth seem particularly excited about or bored by.

Listen Up (30 min)

I'd Dress up for That

Designate one side of the room "sweats and stained tee shirt" and the other side "dressed in my very best." Then ask students to choose a point somewhere along this spectrun to indicate how much they'd dress up for each of the following scenarios:

- First date
- Sitting at home, eating chips, watching TV
- Meet the President
- School
- Awards banquet
- Wedding
- Job interview at McDonald's
- Job interview at the mayor's office
- Homecoming football game
- Court for speeding ticket
- Church

After each choice is made, ask a few students why they chose the spot they did.

Say: *We dress up for important people in our lives, so it seems appropriate to dress up for God. Sure, God accepts us as we are. God loves us if we're covered in filth just as much as when we're wearing a formal dress or a tuxedo. But by dressing up, by making an effort to look nicer than we do every other day, we are sending a message to the world that God is important to us, and that worshiping God is important to us. More importantly, we're telling God, 'You are important to me, God. I want to offer you my best.'*

Dress Up Challenge
Challenge your group to commit to dressing up for church four weeks in a row. If this is too much for your students, reduce the commitment to two weeks, or even one; the important part of this activity is that everyone agrees and participates—even to the point of informing any students not present at this meeting of the plan. The goal for this activity is

Notes:

Notes:

for students to be intentional in preparing for worship. Planning to dress up means thinking about getting prepared for worship for more than five minutes before walking out of the house.

If asked why they dressed up that week, they can respond "Because we dress up for important things, and there's nothing more important than worshiping God."

You may wish to discuss and reach a consensus of what "dressed up" means for your area. In some communities a clean shirt with a collar and sleeves is dressed up, while in other places nothing short of a dress or suit and tie will do. Push your students to go all out in their commitment to this. Oh, and you have to participate too, by the way. That's only fair.

Plan to spend a few minutes after worship on the final week of the commitment to discuss if the students' experience of worship was any different. Who knows, some of your students may like dressing up so much that they decide to do it regularly. Of course, it's fine if this doesn't happen.

Have someone read aloud Psalm 86:8-10.

Explain: *Soren Kierkegaard, a Danish philosopher from the 1800s, said that worship is like a performance; but unlike any other performance we know of. It's not a preacher, choir or worship band on stage, performing for the congregation. Instead, all the worshippers together, preacher, choir, band, soloists, pianist, <u>and</u> everybody in the pews, are the performers... God is the audience.* (Pause for effect.) *Worship is about God, not us.*

What happens in Worship?

Get out your marker and whiteboard or newsprint. Ask your students to try and name, in order, every single thing that happens in a typical Sunday morning worship service at your church. List each element of worship they mention. Leave space for overlooked elements: when someone remembers one, go back and put it in its proper place. Don't correct students as you go. Instead allow time for students to correct one another. Be prepared to do some erasing and reinserting.

When your group thinks they've named everything, point out each element of worship and ask, *"Why do you think we do this?"* Don't correct or comment (other than praising those who venture an answer), but do allow students to comment on one another's answers. When your group thinks they have all elements listed and they have been asked about the reason behind each, pass around the bulletins or copies of the order of worship and ask, *"Is there anything we missed?"* If so, add it in its proper place. Also rearrange anything that was placed out of order.

A Cumberland Presbyterian Service Has...
Look at the following worship service elements. If there are elements mentioned here that are not included in a typical service at your church, go ahead and discuss them and ask students how they feel about their exclusion.

There are no prepared discussion questions in this section, but allow and welcome questions from your students as you explain these various elements of worship. You may want to display the following elements of worship on newsprint or in PowerPoint to give a visual on which students can focus. If desired, use the "notes" section to re-write these descriptions in your own words.

Say: *Worship services are made up of different components— all of which serve a purpose, have a special meaning, or both. We're going to look at each of the components individually:*

- *Prelude. This is music played to help worshippers transition from their ordinary day into being fully focused on worshiping God. The idea is for worshippers to quietly prepare their hearts and minds for the rest of the worship service. The prelude is as much a part of worship as any other and should be treated as such.*

- *Call to Worship. This is someone calling, or inviting, the congregation to enter into worship, emphasizing why we are gathered: to worship God. Usually scripture is used, but sometimes it's a call ("Lift up your hearts") and response ("We lift them to the Lord") between the leader and the congregation.*

- *Praises. We praise God through music, singing, dance, art, and other ways. We don't praise God for what God has done, but for who God is. That means we praise God for being the creator of everything, the giver of all good things, the provider of all that we need, the one who has*

Notes:

Leader Tip:

Some of your students may be familiar with contemporary worship (no bulletins, no hymnals, mostly upbeat music and lots of it, etc.) Some of them may be familiar with blended worship, which combines elements of traditional and contemporary worship. Some congregations see traditional, contemporary and blended worship as all outdated and are trying new forms of worship (some of which, ironically, are actually ancient Christian practices).

Some churches are using worship stations. After a brief time as one body, worshippers move to various stations where they pray, light candles, sing, meditate on scripture, create art based on scripture, walk a prayer labyrinth, receive communion, remember their baptism, read scripture, burn incense, sit in silence before God, or any number of other worshipful activities.

If you are interested in such a thing, you might want to check out *Sacred Space: A Hands-On Guide to Creating Multisensory Worship Experiences for Youth Ministry* by Dan Kimball and Lilly Lewin, Zondervan / Youth Specialties, 2008.

---

saved us from sin and death, the one who sustains us through good times and bad. We do not praise God for what God has done: that's giving thanks. Songs of praise should be about God ("Our God is an Awesome God"; "Holy, Holy, Holy"; "Worship His Majesty", etc.)

- *Opening prayer / prayer of invocation / prayer of adoration.* In this prayer we continue praising God, and we ask God to receive our worship with joy. We may also invoke the Holy Spirit, which means asking that the Holy Spirit come and be present as we worship. This doesn't mean that God does what we say, or that the Holy Spirit won't come if we don't ask; it's just a way of affirming to us and to God that what we do in worship is more about God than us. The invocation happens early in the service because if God isn't present in our worship service, then there's no point in having the service.

- *Confession.* Christians aren't perfect: they're human, so they sin. The difference between Christians and non-Christians is that we have the Holy Spirit dwelling within us to convict us of our sins and call us to confession and repentance. Confession is admitting our sins, repentance is turning away from those sins and back to God. In our personal lives we confess to God, and ask forgiveness for, our personal sins (forgive me for lying to Jill, forgive me for thinking I'm better than Jack). In worship, though, we confess to God, and ask forgiveness for, our sins as a community (forgive us for ignoring the hungry and needy, forgive us for not telling others about Jesus). Some churches include a time for silent personal prayers of confession along with the congregational prayer of confession. The prayer of confession is often preceded by a call to confession in which worshippers are reminded of the need for confession. The prayer is usually followed by an assurance of forgiveness in which worshippers are given assurance that, through Jesus Christ, God forgives them. This assurance is usually followed by an act of praise such as singing the Gloria Patri (Glory be to the Father, and to the Son, and to the Holy Ghost).

- *Listening for God.* Worshippers listen for God in the reading of scripture and in the message (the sermon, or lesson), and sometimes also through song, dance, or drama. The idea here is that God speaks to us both through Holy Scripture and whatever God has inspired the preacher (or singer, actor, and dancer) to say about that *scripture. This is an important element of worship, but is not the most important element of worship; therefore, it should not be treated as any more or any less important than any other element. Every element of worship is equally important and should be treated as such.*

- *Affirmation of Faith. This can be a creed from church history such as the Apostles' Creed or the Nicene Creed; a creed from scripture such as Deuteronomy 6:4-5, 26:5-9, 1 Corinthians 15:3-7, or Philippians 2:6-11; a section from the Confession of Faith; or some other creed written for use in worship. Worshippers affirm their faith by stating what they believe. This serves 1) to remind us of what we believe (we are affirming what we believe by saying it aloud), 2) to summarize for any non-Christians present what Christians believe, 3) to remind us that we are a community rather than just individuals (which is why we say it together), and 4) to serve as a boundary-check for the rest of the service. As we say the affirmation of faith, we are to ask ourselves if everything that was said and done within the service falls within the parameters of the creed; we need to question anything that doesn't.*

- *Prayers of the People / Pastoral Prayer. This is the (usually) long prayer in which the pastor or someone else gives thanks to God for specific blessings from God. (Remember, we thank God for what God has done). In this prayer we also ask God to meet specific needs of the congregation, community, and world. Many congregations conclude this prayer with everybody praying the Lord's Prayer together.*

- *The Offering. This is the time in worship when worshipers specifically and visibly give something back to God. We've already been giving God our worship, of course, but this is a little different. In this portion of the service we acknowledge that everything belongs to God. God gives us a certain things (time, skills, abilities, relationships, money, food, homes, clothes) to take care of and use in the best way possible. The offerings we give back to God are our way of saying thank you, and our way of supporting the ministries of the congregation and denomination. The offerings we offer to God in worship include money, but are not limited to money. This is a good time for worshippers to offer singing ability, musical ability, dancing, or to make a commitment to offer other abilities to be used for God-pleasing purposes (yard work, feeding*

Notes:

Notes:

the hungry, free babysitting, tutoring).

- *Hymns. Singing has been a part of worship as long as people have been worshiping God. In Christian worship, the songs sung by the congregation are called "hymns." Every hymn sung should nicely fit into its portion of the worship service. For example, a hymn of praise ("All Hail the Power of Jesus' Name") would be most appropriate during the praise portion of worship, but a hymn of offering or commitment ("Here I am, Lord") would be most appropriate during the offering portion of worship.*

- *Benediction. This is the Latin word for "blessing" and literally means something like "good (spoken) words." The pastor offers this, on behalf of God, as a parting gift to worshipers. In many churches, though, the benediction is treated like a closing prayer: the pastor asking God's blessings on the congregation instead of blessing the people on behalf of God. The former is more correct, as it harkens back to the blessings we read about in the Old Testament, but the latter is not necessarily incorrect.*

- *Postlude. This music, like the prelude, is as much a part of worship as any other element. It should be used as a time for each worshipper to quietly reflect on what has just happened in worship.*

- *Announcements. Announcements break the flow of worship by drawing attention away from God and back to mundane concerns. Some churches avoid this by making announcements before worship, some by making them after worship, some by printing them in bulletins or on screen... but most churches go ahead and break the flow of worship by including these somewhere within the time that is supposed to be all about God.*

# Now What? (10 min)

Youth Sunday
If your congregation does not have a tradition of the youth group leading worship once a year, encourage your group to ask the session to approve trying this. (Carrying out such a service will take some planning. Be sure to include the senior

pastor in making the request of the session and in determining the exact date for Youth Sunday. You should also inform the senior pastor of anything out of the ordinary you plan to try so that he or she can support you if complaints arise.) Consider having the youth elect two or three representatives to draft a letter making this request and present it to the session.

If an annual youth-led worship service is already a tradition in your congregation, but it's usually exactly like the normal worship service (the only real difference being that youth are leading), then encourage your group to go beyond what they normally do. Plan on at least six meetings (depending on the size of your group) to prepare an innovative youth-led worship service. At the first planning meeting, whip out that video of the "groolest service possible" and ask students how they can make their service like that (assuming there were no live animal sacrifices, pole dancing, or other completely inappropriate things done).

 ## Live It (5 min)

Say: *Worship is about God, not us. Worship is about God, not us. Worship is about God, not us.*

Distribute BOOMM or GROOL handouts and give directions accordingly.

Prayer: *Thank you, God for the gift of worship. May how we worship you, in public and in private, bring you joy. Amen.*

Resources used in creating this lesson: "Directory of Worship" in the *Cumberland Presbyterian Confession of Faith*

©2011 Discipleship Ministry Team of the Ministry Council of the Cumberland Presbyterian Church, All Rights Reserved.

Worship:
BOOMM or GROOL

Take this checklist with you to worship over the next few weeks. When you feel either completely bored or really excited during worship, whip out this sheet and answer the questions below by putting an ✗ in the appropriate ☐.

After worship, reflect on your answers to see what may be causing your boredom or excitement.

Did I take time to prepare my heart and mind for worship today?
    ☐ Yes   ☐ No

Am I focused on God?
    ☐ Fully and completely
    ☐ Some
    ☐ God who?

Am I here to give God something or am I expecting to be entertained?
    ☐ Gimme, gimme, gimme
    ☐ Here I am, Lord; for you.

Am I fully participating in worship (singing, listening, praying, etc.)?
    ☐ Fully and completely
    ☐ Some
    ☐ I'm worshiping like a rock.

Am I sitting near someone who is distracting me?
    ☐ Yes
    ☐ No
    ☐ I'm the one distracting others!

Am I paying attention to the words of the songs as well as the music?
    ☐ Yes   ☐ No

☐ **I'm BOOMM (Bored Out OF My Mind)!**

☐ **This Worship Service is GROOL (Great + Cool)!**

Notes:

No Harm Done, It's Just for Fun!

By Andy McClung

Scripture: 1 Corinthians 10:23

Theme: Our entertainment choices have a lasting effect on us, whether or not we realize it. This lesson helps students develop critical thinking skills and consider the long-range effects of their entertainment choices.

Resource List

- Index cards—one per student
- Copies of "No Harm Done, It's Just for Fun" handout for each student

Leader Prep

- Print on each index card one of the following behaviors or activities: going to the movies, dancing, playing a game of cards, being gay, homosexual activity, drinking alcohol, masturbating, not playing with venomous snakes, being Roman Catholic, abortion, not being Caucasian, getting a tattoo, wearing makeup, shopping on Sunday, girls having short hair. Fold each card in half and staple or tape it so that it cannot be easily read. If you have more students than topics listed here, it's okay to duplicate these activities.
- Three signs made from regular printer paper. One should read "sin," one "not a sin," and the third should have a question mark on it. Tape these signs to the walls in your meeting space, leaving plenty of space in between them.
- (Optional) Ask students to bring to this meeting some of their favorite music. Make sure you have a way to play the music in multiple media (CDs, MP3, etc.).
- Pray for the church universal, your students, their families, advertisers, the entertainment industry, and yourself as you prepare to lead this lesson.

Leader Insights

Connecting to Your Students

Just as we need to prepare the resources for a lesson, we need to prepare our hearts and minds for the Biblical and theological insights each lesson provides. Familiarize yourself

Notes:

with these insights to help you respond to the discussion questions and activities throughout the lesson.

Your job in this lesson is not to chastise your students about their poor entertainment choices, nor to disparage youth culture at large. Such comments serve only to close down, rather than open up, communication. Neither is your job in this lesson to instill in your students an "anything goes and nothing really matters" attitude toward entertainment. Your job in this lesson is to teach your students to think critically about the entertainment choices they make.

Lesson Background
In today's lesson we will be exploring cultural media—movies, songs, commercials—and its impact on our lives. In one of the activities students will be sharing about movies they have seen. If you have not seen a movie which your students mention and want to discuss, ask someone to summarize the story. Listen for two of the most common themes in Hollywood productions: revenge (which is pursued by the hero, and usually portrayed simply as what has to be done, with no ethical concerns or mention of the possibility of forgiveness), and love (eros, the romantic type of love between a man and a woman) being able to overcome any obstacle or difficulty. Neither of these lessons is true or good, and can lead to a warped and unrealistic idea of how life should be.

Don't argue about a work's inherent message, but don't gloss over the negative or conflicting messages within any particular media piece either. The point of the lesson is for your students to learn how to analyze the things they consume for entertainment. Note that for print media (magazines and websites) your approach needs to be a bit different. For these, point out how the writer can manipulate words to obscure some facts and highlight others while maintaining an appearance of neutrality, and how the writer may be blatantly trying to influence what the reader thinks about the topic.

In 1956 Richard Niebuhr published <u>Christ and Culture</u> in which he proposes five possible relationships between Christians and the culture in which they live. In North America entertainment is a huge part of culture.

Niebuhr says Christians can be **against culture**. These are the persons who seem to find no value in anything other than specifically God-oriented activities and who may even see all secular entertainment as ungodly. Or, Christians may be in

agreement with culture, finding pathways to Christ within certain elements of culture.

Christians can see Christ as being **above culture**, separating life into the parts that are appropriate for spiritual activities and the parts that are purely secular. Christians with this mindset may see no problem with, say, lying as part of a business transaction because business and religion have nothing to do with each other; one is earthly and the other is spiritual. Other Christians, says Niebuhr, see their Christianity **in paradox with culture**. They see humankind as bound to worldly (sinful) things, such as culture, but called to sacred things by God.

Niebuhr's final relationship holds up Christ as the one who **transforms culture** from something bad into something good. Christians, as the Body of Christ, are to strive to transform culture themselves. This mindset holds that culture was originally good, but corrupted by sin. The Christian's duty, then, is to redeem culture in Christ's name.

Working with youth in an entertainment-saturated culture, perhaps the best approach for youth ministry workers is to stand with Niebuhr's final option: seeing the Christian's job as transforming culture from something corrupted by sin, back into its original goodness that points to God. And that is the point of this lesson: not to denigrate something that is a huge part of your students' lives, but to take the first steps in teaching them to reflect on, think deeply about, and draw beneficial conclusions about what they consume in the name of entertainment.

Media

Looking beyond the glitz to discern what a movie teaches—whether subtly or overtly—is not that difficult. It does, however, take an intentional effort. Some of the most popular war movies actually have anti-war messages. Some movies that glamorize pornography or casual sex actually have responsible sex messages. Sometimes, though, the lesson is not within the movie, but the simple fact that the movie exists. For example, an ultra-violent, eye candy movie such as Crank 2: High Voltage may have no imbedded lesson, but its very existence puts forth the message that violence and gore are entertaining. It's not uncommon for a movie to send two or more contradictory messages. The 40-Year Old Virgin is an example of this. It seems to teach that abstaining from sex before marriage is a good and healthy thing to do, even if one

Notes:

Leader Tip:

War movies with anti-war messages: Platoon (1986), Starship Troopers (1997). Sex-themed movie with anti-casual sex messages: The Girl Next Door (2004).

has to wait until the age of 40, but the movie also teaches that sex outside of marriage is okay under the right circumstances.

Some Christians, it seems, are always on the lookout for the next thing they can be angry about. One would think Christians are supposed to be <u>for</u> Jesus more than they are <u>against</u> anything of this world, but history speaks for itself. In the 1800's The Temperance Movement preached that alcohol was the most evil thing in the world. In the 1980's, many Christians were convinced that playing Dungeons and Dragons would lead kids straight into demonic possession. In the early 2000s it was Harry Potter, whose exploits were surely leading kids to practice sorcery. And it seems the more popular something is in the secular world, the louder these Christians disparage it.

One of the great things about the Judeo-Christian tradition is that God loves us so much that he cares about every little aspect of our lives. God spelled out in the Old Testament how to do just about everything imaginable, from the big stuff in the Ten Commandments to seemingly insignificant things such as how to clean pots and pans before cooking with them. This level of detail was unheard of in ancient religions.

Some Christians have taken God's guidelines for life and decided that it's their job to insure everyone in the world abides by them. Worse, they have decided that any behavior which might possibly even lead to sin is sinful itself. That's why some Christians have decided that dancing is sinful: they fear it will lead to sex.

Theological Underpinnings
Judaism put a lot of emphasis on rules. There are actually 613 laws in the Old Testament. Jesus pretty much replaced all of those when he said the two most important commandments are loving "the Lord your God with all your heart, and with all your soul, and with all your mind" and loving "your neighbor as yourself" (Matt. 22:37-40).

Some people like having everything spelled out for them ("It's okay to do this, but not that") more than they like making decisions for themselves. This was the attitude Paul was dealing with in the early church. Some people wanted Christianity to be like Judaism; they had been taught that the only way to please God was to follow all 613 rules perfectly. Doing so, however, was next to impossible and surely led a great many people to feeling hopeless about ever actually pleasing God. Those who had not grown up Jewish needed to know what was and what wasn't allowed in this new way of living called Christianity. Some people today still want someone -- God, the Bible, Jesus, the pastor -- to declare what's not allowed so they can focus all their energy on not doing that. But constantly being in fear of breaking the rules is not the best way to live out one's faith.

Those who follow the way of Jesus, Paul would say, are to focus on doing good things instead of focusing on not doing bad things. If you're putting everything you have into loving God and neighbor, then you're probably not going to be doing any of those things that God doesn't want us doing. In 1 Corinthians 10:23 Paul is saying that we can tell the difference between what's good to do and what's bad to do by whether or not it builds us up, or benefits us, depending on the translation you're using.

Applying the Lesson to Your own Life
What's your favorite form of entertainment? When consuming secular entertainment, how much thought do you give to the messages in it? Think about the last TV show you watched or book you read for fun. What were some positive messages in it? What were some negative messages in it?

Think back to when you were about your students' age. What entertainment do you remember as being labeled bad or harmful by some Christians? Did you agree or disagree with them back then? Did you consume (read, play, listen to, watch) it? Do you agree with them now?

Do you think entertainment produced by Christians can carry harmful messages when it promotes the idea that with enough faith, all Christians can lead happy and trouble-free lives? What form of entertainment would you most like to see Christ transform?

Notes:

Leader Tip:

Expect, of course, smart aleck answers such as "Don't steal from mobsters" and "Don't get lost in woods where psycho cannibal hillbillies live." Also expect some students to say that a particular movie wasn't meant to teach anything, but simply to entertain. Hold firm, though, that every movie teaches us something. Hopefully, you have seen—or at least are familiar with—some of the movies your students mention and will be able to reveal what the movie teaches. Example: The *Twilight* movies teach teen girls that it's romantic to have a boyfriend who could lose control at any moment and kill you. *Rise of the Planet of the Apes* teaches that messing with nature can lead to serious consequences.

The Lesson

 # Get Started (15 min)

Is This a Sin?

Give each student one of the cards you've prepared, instructing him or her not to open it. Explain that when you say "go," the students are to read what's written on their cards and move to one of three points, indicated by your signs. Any student who thinks what's written on his or her card is a sin is to stand as close as possible to the "sin" sign. Any student who thinks what's written on his or her card is not a sin is to stand as close as possible to the "not a sin" sign. Anyone who can't decide may go to the question mark sign. What students may not do is reveal to anyone else what their cards say, or ask for help deciding.

When all students have chosen a spot, tell those at the question mark that they may ask either group -- but not both groups – for help deciding. For example, a student holding "drinking alcohol" is standing at the question mark because she can't decide if it's a sin or not. She may ask <u>either</u> the group standing at the "sin" sign <u>or</u> the group standing at the "not a sin" sign if they think drinking alcohol is a sin. She may not ask both groups. After hearing the responses, she must choose to move to either "sin" or "not a sin." Encourage each student at the question mark to seek advice and make a final choice. If all of your students go straight to the question mark, encourage some to make a decision. If none will, eliminate the question mark as an option.

Ask a few students why they made the choices they did. If you have students at each sign, alternate between the two groups. It may be interesting to ask why those originally at the question mark sign chose one group over another to ask for help in deciding.

Tell your students to swap cards with someone. Give no instructions on how to do this.

When everyone has a new card, explain that you're going to repeat the game, but with one change.

Say: *Read your new card. If you think some group of Christians has ever said that the behavior or activity written on your card is a sin, then move to the 'sin' sign. If you don't think any group of Christians has ever said the activity written on your card is a sin, then move to the 'not a sin' sign. If you just can't decide, go to the question mark.*

After all have chosen, allow those at the question mark to ask for help deciding, maintaining the restriction of asking only one group.

When everyone is at either the "sin" or the "not a sin" sign, reveal that every single one of these behaviors or activities has been considered a sin by some group of Christians.

Listen Up (25 min)

Go around the room and ask each student to read his or her card.

Discussion Question:
- Which of these behaviors or activities do you think it's ridiculous to consider a sin? Why?

Say: *At some point in time, well-meaning Christians have considered all sorts of stuff to be sinful. Basically, anything that's not churchy has been considered sinful by some Christian group at one time or other. Some of these so-called sins may seem harmless to us now, but in the past, anything that might distract someone from thinking about God or Jesus was considered sinful—well, anything except working to provide for your family or the community.*

Discussion Questions:
- What was the last movie you watched?
- What did it try to teach you?

Say: *Looking beyond the glitz to discern what a movie teaches—whether subtly or overtly—is not that difficult. It does, however, take an intentional effort.*

Ask these questions again, using television shows, music, magazines, websites, video games, and whatever else your

Notes:

> **Leader Tip:**
>
> If you need to help the debate along, ask a few leading questions of those who say entertainment choices do have a lasting effect. (*i.e.* Can you say more about that? Is that effect good or bad? Which kind of entertainment affects you more, a movie or a song?)

students use for entertainment. This is the appropriate time to play and discuss some of the music that students brought to the meeting. Ask them to think about the messages within these things. You may need to shape and guide the conversation to stay on track. Be especially careful to point out or draw out positive messages as well as negative ones so that your students do not become defensive.

Discussion Question:
- Do you think what you do for fun—movies, music, TV, magazines, video games, websites, etc.—affects you beyond just entertaining you for a while?

Presumably, some of your students will answer "yes" and some will answer "no." If so, ask students giving opposite answers to debate, but not argue, with one another. That means each side explains why it is right and the other is wrong without resorting to personal attacks or insults.

Ask the students who think they are immune to media messages: *What about advertising? Do you think companies would spend billions and billions of dollars on advertising every year if they weren't absolutely sure it affects your behavior?*

Questions:
- What we eat and drink affects our bodies (whether we're eating for fun or for health) right?
- The information we see, read, and hear affects our minds (one word: school), right?
- Doesn't it make sense that whatever we consume in the name of entertainment also affects us?

Have someone read aloud 1 Corinthians 10:23.

Discussion Question:
- What do you think Paul is saying in this passage?

Allow any answers without judgment. After students have answered, draw from the background material to explain the shift from Judaism's many laws to Christianity's simpler and more positive approach.

Say: *Maybe what Paul is saying is that we can tell the difference between what's good to do and what's bad to do by whether or not it strengthens our relationship with Christ.*

Discussion Question:
- What do you think would work better at school: being told "Don't steal stuff from other people, don't cheat on tests, don't copy someone else's homework, don't talk back to the teachers, don't run in the hallways, don't damage school property, don't get to class late, don't damage other people's property", or to be told "Do your best work and treat others with respect"?

Say: What Jesus did was replace 613 'don'ts' with two 'dos.' This puts a lot more responsibility on us, but it also frees us from feeling like we can never measure up to all those rules. When Paul wrote, 'I have the right to do anything,' you say—but not everything is beneficial. 'I have the right to do anything'—but not everything is constructive," (1 Corinthians 10:23 TNIV) he didn't mean that Christians have the right to lie, steal, cheat, maim, and kill without consequence, but that the ultra-stringent and super-detailed Hebrew law didn't matter as much as following Jesus' commandments to love God and neighbor with everything we have.

Now What? (10 min)

Transforming Culture

As a group or in small groups discuss the following questions.

Discussion Questions:
- How can we re-purpose media for God's good?
- What movies, songs, or commercials send the Godliest messages?
- What cultural message do you want to pray for God to transform the most?

Notes:

Notes:

 # Live It (5 min)

Pass around copies of "No Harm Done, It's Just for Fun" and challenge your students to continue thinking about their entertainment choices. You may even want to arrange a movie night in which you watch a particular movie as a group and then sit down over pizza and discuss the messages within the movie.

Prayer: *Thank you, God for making human being so creative. Thank you for giving us so many entertainment choices. Help us to truly think about what we put into our minds and spirits in the name of entertainment. Guide us toward things that build us up rather than confuse us or harm us, and give us the strength to say no to harmful entertainment. Amen.*

Resources used in creating this lesson: *Christ and Culture* by Richard Niebuhr.

©2011 Cumberland Presbyterian Church and CYMT Press, All Rights Reserved.

No Harm Done, It's Just For Fun!

This week, pay attention to the entertainment you consume, and answer these questions for each of the following types of entertainment. At the end of the week consider what Jesus would say to you if he looked over your choices!

♪♫♬ Music ♬♫♪

Artist and Song:_____

I like this song because_____

When I really listen to the words, I think this song may be saying_____

_____

☐ I agree with this message and think it's good to learn.

☐ I disagree with this message because_____

_____

🎬 Movies 🎬

Title:_____

What I liked/didn't like about this movie_____

_____

One of the things this movie may be trying to teach me is_____

_____

☐ I agree with this message because_____

_____

☐ I disagree with this message.

🎮 Video Games 🎮

Title:_____

I like to play this game because_____

This game teaches me_____
_____

☐ I think this is a good thing to learn because_____

☐ I don't think this is a good thing to learn.

📺 TV Show 📺

Title:_____

I spend time watching this show because _____

A message I found in this episode was_____

☐ Hearing this message makes a better person by_____
_____

☐ Hearing this message does not make me a better person.

📖 Magazine 📖

Title:_____

I spent some of my day reading this magazine because _____
_____

The people who make this magazine may be trying to teach me___
_____

☐ I agree with this message and am thankful someone wants to teach it to me.

☐ I disagree with this message and wonder why someone would want to teach it to me.

Notes:

Job, Career, or Call: What's the Difference?

By Andy McClung

Scripture: Colossians 1:9-14

Theme: Discerning and following God's will for our lives is known as discovering our vocation, and it's far more important than choosing a career.

Resource List

- sticky nametags or mailing labels, or index cards and tape, one per student
- A whiteboard. If you don't have a big one in your meeting room, a small one designed to hang on the wall will do.
- A few permanent markers and a couple of dry-erase markers, all of the same color
- A few dry paper towels or a whiteboard erase
- Rubbing Alcohol
- Simple (fun size candy bar, a peppermint or other piece of hard candy) and silly (crazy straw, shoelaces, sample-size dental floss) prizes, enough to give one of each to every student (You will have half of these left over.)
- CD (or other music source) of peaceful, meditative music or nature sounds and a way to play it

 ## Leader Prep

Using the index cards, nametags, or mailing labels print different careers from the lists below. Create one card per student. If you have more than 20 students, just repeat some of the careers, but do so evenly from each list. If you have fewer than 20 students, just choose which careers you want to use, but draw evenly from each list.

List #1

Mining Engineer
Metallurgic Engineer
Marine Engineer
Electrical Engineer
Chemical Engineer
Aerospace Engineer
Computer Scientist
Pharmacist
Petroleum Engineer

List #2

Health Professional
Artist
Speech Therapist
Actor/Director
Social Worker
Community Organizer
Pastor
Teacher
Counselor/Psychologist

These lists are based on a 2011 *Time* magazine article that dealt with starting salaries for recent college graduates with degrees in these majors. All those vocations from List #1 (above) are in the higher paid group and all those from List #2 (above) are in the less paid group.

Pray for the Holy Spirit to be active during this lesson.

Notes:

Leader Insights

Connecting to Your Students

Just as we need to prepare the resources for a lesson, we need to prepare our hearts and minds for the Biblical and theological insights each lesson provides. Familiarize yourself with these insights to help you respond to the discussion questions and activities throughout the lesson.

When middle school and high school students think about their future career, they think about what would be fun to do. When college students think about their future careers, they think about what will make enough money to pay off their student loans. What few students think about, it seems, is what God is calling them to do in their future careers.

Chances are, if your students have ever even heard the phrase 'the call of God' in church, it's only been in reference to God calling someone to pursue ordained ministry. That is a deficit within the Protestant Church, but nothing new.

Explaining the Lesson

Christians have done plenty of embarrassingly bad stuff over the last 2,000 years, some of which keeps some people from following Jesus to this day. One of the worst was the development of clericalism. This is the idea that clergy are some kind of special class of Christians who are holier than lay persons and should have more privilege and power than the laity. 'Cleric' is an old-fashioned word for minister; thus the word 'clericalism.' Under this mindset, ministry became something only the clergy did while the laypeople watched and supported them with prayers and money. Clericalism took ministry out of the hands of the people and made it the domain of the clergy alone. Judging from what we see of the early church in the New Testament, however, it was never God's intention for the church to be like this.

Nobody knows who started clericalism, but both the clergy and the laity had to play along to keep it going. Apparently, clergy liked being in control and the laity liked paying someone else to do the ministries of the church.

The Protestant Reformation gave a pretty serious beat down to clericalism, but sadly, vestiges of it are still around in the Protestant church. Perhaps the most prominent place we can still see its affect is in the way we talk about God's 'call as if the only thing God calls people to is ordained ministry. The truth that clericalism obscures, though, is that God calls all Christians to specific professions or careers, which is why we call them vocations (see the sidebar). This lesson explores vocation and call. As you read through the lesson think of ways you can talk with your students about your own sense of vocation.

Theological Underpinnings

The world tells us that the perfect job for a person is either the one that makes him or her happiest, or the one that makes him or her the most money. God seems to consider the perfect job for a person to be the one through which he or she could help the most people, do the most good, and bring the most glory to God through Christ.

God's ways often seem backwards from a worldly perspective: love your enemy, turn the other cheek, asking God to forgive those who harm you, giving away the first and best of your herd or crop... or the first ten percent of your earnings. God calls all Christians to do ministry within their vocations; God calls some Christians to minister as their vocations. We call those in this last group clergy.

Applying the Lesson to Your Own Life

How did you come to be teaching youth, was it in answer to God's call? If you're tempted to answer "no," keep in mind that God calls people in a variety of ways: scripture, the words of a friend, a tugging at the heart or mind, an unexpected opportunity arising. God calls in distinct and undeniable ways as well; many who have been called by God report actually hearing a voice that no on eels could hear. What usually happens is that there is some human agent (friend, spouse, pastor, the church) who helps persons hear or affirm God's call upon their lives. Was there someone who told you that you should teach, or did you already think so and someone affirmed it?

The old saying is true: God doesn't call the equipped, God equips the called. How have you been equipped to answer the call to teach youth? Do you need to talk to the church session about specific training? Do you know that the CP Church now certifies youth ministers?

Notes:

Leader Tip:

"Vocation" comes from the Latin word which means "to call" and literally means "a calling." Christians were the first to use the term, and it referred to God calling a person to some specific action or course of action.

Leader Tip:

In the Pay Scale activity, help your students realize that those careers requiring math and science skills are higher paid while those that overtly and directly help people in need are among the lowest paid. Consider discussing why this might be.

The Lesson

Get Started (12 min)

What Do I Do?

Instruct your students to stand in a circle, facing in. Go around the outside of the circle, taping a career card onto each student's back. Assign cards randomly, but use an equal number from each list.

Say: *The card on your back indicates your career for this game, but you are not to look at it and nobody is going to read it to you. When I give the signal, you are to mingle and ask each other questions about your careers. When you think you know your career, come and stand with your back to this wall.*

Indicate a wall or other place where students can line up. Explain that the question-and-answer exchanges should only produce hints. Not: "What do I do?" "You're a firefighter"; but: "Is my job dangerous?" "It depends on what happens during your shift, but it can be very dangerous." Responses shouldn't include any of the words on the card. Make sure everyone understands, then give your go signal.

When all students think they know their careers, have each one, in turn, stand before the group and say, "Hello, my name is _____. I'm a / an _____", and then remove the career card from his or her back and stick it on his or her chest, revealing it to the group. Give a simple prize to everyone who gets it right and a silly prize to those who get it wrong.

When everyone has had a turn standing before the group, ask the group to keep their cards stuck to their chests and be seated.

Listen Up (30 min)

Discussion Questions:
- What do you want to be when you grow up?
- What does God want you to be?
- How are these questions different?
- What do you think when you hear the word, 'vocation'?

Explain: *"Vocation" comes from the Latin word which means "to call" and literally means "a calling." Christians were the first to use the term, and it referred to God calling a person to some specific action or course of action.*

Discussion Questions:
- What do you think when you hear the word 'call' or 'calling'?
- Who is called?

Say: *God calls all Christians to do ministry within their professions. The Twitter version of this theology could be: God calls all Christians to minister within their vocations; God calls some to minister as their vocations, and these we call clergy.*

Pay Scale

Ask your students to separate themselves into two groups based on the career cards stuck to their chests: one group is the higher paid careers and the other is the less paid. Indicate a different point in your meeting space for each group to gather. Students are free to choose for themselves, ask advice of their peers, and offer advise to one naother, but everyone must choose on eof the two groups.

After everyone has chosen a group, reveal the correct groupings using the lists above.

Ask anyone in the wrong group to move to the correct group, and then ask your students to look around at the career cards, taking note of the kinds of careers in their group and the careers in the other group.

Notes:

Notes:

Discussion Questions:
- What do you notice about how these careers are grouped?
- Does this seem how God would want things to be?
- If not, then why is it this way?

Say: *The world says the more money it makes, the better the job. But God seems to think that the best job for anybody is the one through which he or she can help the most people, do the most good, and bring the most glory to God through Christ.*

The world tells us to choose a career based on what makes us happy or what can earn us the most money, but God wants us to listen for the career he is calling us to and then follow that call whether or not it makes us happy or earns us any money.

But it's not easy to hear God's call, is it?

Obfuscation
Have each student write his or her name on the whiteboard using a permanent marker if your whiteboard is big enough or your group small enough. Each name will need a few inches of blank space around it. If you don't have this kind of space or your group is too large, choose a few students to write their names on the whiteboard using the permanent markers. You may choose randomly, but if you know your students well enough to know that some learn best by visual artistic expressions, choose them.

When students are done, gather the permanent markers. Point to the names written on the board and say: *This is you, the person God intends for you to be: all your hopes, dreams, relationships, skills, gifts, and abilities; your personality, the things that bring you joy, the things that make you laugh. This is you.*

Take your time with this, as you need the marker ink to dry thoroughly onto the whiteboard.

Using dry-erase markers the same color as the permanent markers—slowly scribble over the names as you say: *But all sorts of things happen in your life that keep you from fully becoming the person God means for you to be.Tthings like: your parents' expectations of you, wanting a certain lifestyle more than wanting to follow God's will, thinking that money is the most important thing in making decisions, trying to impress people, being indecisive, wanting to be popular, wanting people to like you, taking the easy way, making poor choices in who your friends are, circumstances beyond your control, and all sorts of other stuff.*

You don't have to completely obfuscate the name, but make it close.

Step away from the board so the students can see the obfuscated names, and say: *So, sooner or later, it comes to the point where you might have a career going, or you're in college... but whether your life is going well or going poorly, it's not really <u>you</u>, you're not being the person God intended you to be, you're not doing with your life what God wants. The real you has been covered up, hidden by all these other things.*

Step back to the whiteboard with the eraser, cloth, or paper towels and slowly begin wiping away the dry-erase marker to reveal the names written in permanent marker.

Say: *Our lesson today is about finding out who God intends you to be, and following that call, before all this other stuff gets in the way.*

(You can clean the whiteboard later using specialized cleaner or rubbing alcohol.)

Say: *Some people spend their whole lives trying to discern what God is calling them to do. Some hear God's call too late in their lives to change careers easily. Some have careers that make enough money to feed their families, but still figure out ways to follow their vocations as well. And some follow their vocation, their call, as their career.*

Following God's call to pursue your vocation is not always easy. It may mean doing something that scares you, or something you think you're unqualified for, or something really dangerous. It may mean going against your parents' wishes and expectations for you. It may mean doing the exact opposite of what you always wanted to do.

But once a person discerns and follows God's call upon their lives, the sense of satisfaction and the feelings of peace and rightness with God have no comparison.

Notes:

Notes:

Discussion Questions:
- How do we discern what vocation God is calling us to?
- How do we hear God's call?

Say: *We have to listen. God speaks to us through the Bible, through the faith community (the church universal and fellow believers), and sometimes even directly through our prayers.*

Examples:
In Colossians 1:9-14, the Apostle Paul describes what happens when we know and follow God's call: we live a life that is truly worth something and that is pleasing to God; we learn as we go; we grow to know better and better how God does things; and we experience joy.

In Galatians 2:20, Paul nicely sums up what it means for a believer fully to follow God's call: "It is no longer I who live, but Christ who lives within me."

Choose one of the Biblical stories of call from the handout that means a lot to you and share it with the group. If you feel led to, share your own story of call and vocation now.

Affirmations (Optional) (15 min)
Play the affirmations game. Break your group up into groups of six to eight students and at least one adult. Have groups sit in circles throughout the room. Start with one student and have all the other students affirm how they see God in that person. For example, a student might share, "I see God in you because you're such a good friend". No other talking should be allowed.

Obviously, this exercise is risky for the shy students. They will know that if it's managed poorly it will embarrass them or make them feel even more awkward. So, manage it well.

The hope of this exercise is to help the person being affirmed to start thinking about his or her spiritual gifts, so try to guide the comments more along the lines of "I see God in the way you explain things so that it is easy to understand," rather than "I see God in how you're so smart." Try to steer your students away from superficial compliments to things that really matter.

It may help if you, the leader, take the first turn being

affirmed. You may also need to rephrase some of the comments to set the proper tone, but try to stay out of it as much as possible. Praise from peers beats praise from the youth leader any day.

Close this exercise by thanking everyone for participating and explain: *Many, many people will tell you that they never would have heard God's call without the help of other believers. Sometimes this help came through the writing or preaching or teaching of a fellow Christian whom they'd never met, sometimes through intense one-on-one counseling, sometimes through a casual comment, sometimes through a fellow believer praying for the person to hear God's call, and sometimes through other ways involving fellow Christians. Those who have discerned God's call upon their lives will almost always say that there was someone, a fellow believer, who affirmed that call.*

Now What? (10 min)

Prayerful Listening
Turn on the meditative music and explain that you're going to lead the group in a time of prayer.
Say: *Prayer is supposed to be how we communicate with God, right? But how often do we stop talking and listen as we pray? If we walk up to a friend and talk nonstop for a few minutes, and then walk away before he or she could say anything, we wouldn't consider that a conversation would we? Effective communication requires speaking and listening. Effective prayer does too. Even when we ask God to reveal things to us, to help us make decisions, we rarely stop to listen for God's responses. It may very well be that we should spend far more time listening that talking when we pray.*

Pray something like, "*Thank you, God, for calling each of us into a relationship with you through Jesus. For those in this room who haven't yet established that relationship, we ask that you move them to do so soon. For those who have, we ask that you speak to them now, open their hearts and minds to your Holy Spirit who reveals your will for their lives, extends to them your call upon their lives, and reveals to them the spiritual gifts you have placed within them and what you want them to do with those gifts...*"

Just in Case

There may be some strong reactions to this lesson. Some students may feel called to pursue ordained ministry, some may feel called to international mission work. If you are not qualified to counsel them on such matters, have in mind someone who is, so you can refer them.

Some students may have picked up on the language used in the lesson hinting that a saving relationship with God through Christ precedes God's call to vocation. Invite students who have not yet made a profession of faith to speak with you further about this, and be prepared for discussions about the difference between coming to church and youth group and professing faith in Jesus as Lord and Savior.

Bear in mind that adoles-cence is a tumultuous time. The days of carefree childhood and living for the day are dwindling, and youth know it. Serious decisions with lifelong ramifications are just around the corner. Your students know they need solid spiritual guidance, even if they don't want to admit it. Helping them follow God's call instead of the world's call is one of the greatest and longest lasting gifts you can give them.

Notes:

Then enter a time of silence. If you're not used to doing this you might want to use a watch, as a few seconds of silence can seem like several minutes. Most people are comfortable with only twenty seconds of silence. You should plan to utilize at least three to five minutes of silence. Plan the music accordingly.

Close the time of silence by praying something like, *"Thank you, God, for revealing yourself and your will to us. Continue to call each of us so that we may do with our lives what you want us to. Amen"*

After the "amen," explain that we don't always hear God when we try to, especially if we are distracted or resistant. Encourage your students to incorporate a period of listening in their regular prayer time. If you do not have a period of silence in Sunday morning worship, ask your students if they think it'd be a good idea to suggest to the pastor or worship team that one be included.

 ## Live It (5 min)

Read aloud Colossians 1:9-14.

Ask: Who feels God calling you to close our meeting with a prayer?

If no one feels so called, pass out the 'Job, Career, or Call' handout and dismiss the meeting. Do not pray the closing prayer yourself.

This may seem radical, but you may even want to incorporate this method at the end of every meeting. The youth leader closing every meeting with prayer supports clericalism, whether or not you are seeking ordination.

Resources used in creating this lesson: The Once and Future Church by Loren Mead, Westminster Dictionary of Theological Terms edited by Don McKim, dictionary.com

©2011 Discipleship Ministry Team of the Ministry Council of the Cumberland Presbyterian Church, All Rights Reserved.

Job, Career, or Call: What's the Difference?

Job: Something done to make money that can be full time or part time, short term or long term. Minimal training or education necessary.

Career: An occupation or profession, usually full time and long term (even life long). Likely requires specialized and extensive training or education.

Call: What God wants you to do with your life. This may or may not be your career. It may not seem to make sense to you or those who love you. It probably will not be easy. It will make use of your God-given gifts (abilities), including those you may not know you have. It will involve living a Christ-like life. Following your call will be the most rewarding thing you've ever experienced.

Call Stories in the Bible

This week, read some of the stories in the Bible about God calling persons to specific vocations. Pray before you read that God will speak to you. Pray after you read as well, but leave plenty of time to remain silent before God so you can listen for God. Remember, God doesn't always speak to us with a booming voice from the sky or a burning bush. Sometimes it's a tugging in your heart or an unexpected thought in your mind. Sometimes it's through the words of a friend, the preacher, or even a complete stranger.

- God calls Abram in Genesis 12.
- God calls Moses in Exodus 3:1-4:18.
- God calls Isaiah in Isaiah 6:1-9.
- God calls Jeremiah in Jeremiah 4:1-10
- God calls Saul (Paul) in Acts 9:1-3.
- Jesus calls Simon, Andrew, James, and John in Matthew 4:18-22.

Notice that in these stories:
- God's call isn't necessarily what the called person would have chosen to do.
- Following God's call often involves struggle, hardship, and sacrifice.
- God accomplished amazing things through the lives of those who heard and answered God's call.

Finish this sentence: Sometimes I think God might be calling me to

_____

_____

Can Preachers Wear High Heels?
By Andy McClung

Scripture: Galatians 3:27-28

Theme: God calls both men and women into ministry. The Cumberland Presbyterian Church ordains women as ministers. This lesson guides students in considering scriptural support for women.

Resource List

- Treats—If you have someone in the church who makes a particular dessert for potluck meals that's a favorite of the youth, contact him or her and ask for more than enough of the treat for everyone in the group. If you do not have such a person in your church, bring some homemade goodies that are sure to please. If that's impossible as well, bring some store-bought goodies, enough for everyone in the group.
- Copies of the handout 'Can Preachers Wear High Heels?' for each student. Note: This week's handout is two pages. Copy double-sided if possible.
- Pens and paper

Leader Prep

- Pre-arrange with one of the girls in your group to pray the closing prayer.
- Pray for your students during the week leading up to this lesson, asking that the Holy Spirit lead them into conversations and situations that bring gender expectations to mind, especially within the church.

Leader Insights

Connecting to Your Students

Just as we need to prepare the resources for a lesson, we need to prepare our hearts and minds for the Biblical and theological insights each lesson provides. Familiarize yourself with these insights to help you respond to the discussion questions and activities throughout the lesson.

Teens are still trying to figure out what they believe about gender roles. Their ideas are influenced to some degree by personal observation and the media, but the primary influence on these ideas is what they hear and see at home. This influence cuts two ways, though. Teens who are outspoken in their views of gender roles may be echoing their parents, or they might be rebelling against their parents' ideals. Rest assured that what to expect from the opposite gender, and of themselves, in adulthood is one of the many things that teens wonder and worry about.

A personal note from the writer:

I was quite confused about the issue of women in ministry myself once upon a time. I was unsure if it was truly a God thing, or a merely response to cultural changes. A few rude and outspoken women of various denominations who were preparing for ministry or already ordained and who seemed to hate men as much as they loved Jesus almost swayed me against women in ministry. A good bit of prayerful listening, and reading Lousia Woosley's book, *Shall Woman Preach? Or The Question Answered*, however, made me realize that God does indeed call both men and women to be ministers, and he's been doing so a long time.

Explaining the Lesson

Different cultures have had different ideas of what is appropriate for men, what is appropriate for women, what is inappropriate for men, and what is inappropriate for women. We call these ideas gender roles or gender expectations. In most cultures throughout history, these roles have been well-established and have gone unchanged for long periods of time. In western culture (that of Western Europe and North America), however, these roles have experienced considerable change in the last century, and dramatic change in the last few decades. One of those changes is that more and more women have entered professions previously considered men's territory. This includes ordained ministry.

Long before there were the dozens of different Christian denominations we have today, there was just one denomination, one Christian church: the Roman Catholic Church. In Roman Catholicism ordination is reserved for men alone because the priest represents Jesus and Jesus was a man. Roman Catholics, though, did and still do recognize the importance of women in the church. There are several orders of nuns who do an incredible amount of ministry in this world. Ordination to the priesthood, however, is still reserved for men alone.

When the Protestant Church was born by the Protestant Reformation, the floodgates opened and today we have many different denominations. The Reformation happened because some church leaders, such as Martin Luther, disagreed with certain teachings and practices of the Roman Catholic Church (none of which, however, was the fact that women could not be priests).

Today, some denominations ordain women as ministers and some do not. Some of those which do not ordain women claim that they base their refusal to do so on scripture. Those who think women should not be in ministry seem to focus on just two or three of the Bible's 30,000 or so verses to support their argument.

In 1 Corinthians 14:34, Paul says women should be silent in church. This, some people say, means a woman shouldn't preach. It's interesting, though, that the same people who want to take this particular verse so literally don't take other verses as literally: love your enemies (Matthew 5:44), cut off your hand if it causes you to sin (Mark 9:43), don't eat pork or catfish (Leviticus 11:7-8, 10). Even those who agree with Paul's words about women staying silent in church, however, don't follow those words literally. If they did, then they would keep women from saying *anything* in church: no teaching Sunday school, no singing in the choir, no singing hymns with the congregation, no welcoming visitors, no answering the questions for church membership, no making announcements... nothing. Silent means silent. But nobody says all that. They seem to think this silence applies only to preaching, even though Paul sets no such parameters. It's also interesting that those who hold so tightly to Paul's words about women remaining silent in church seem not to notice that just a few verses earlier, in 14:26, Paul says that each member of the faith community has something to offer when they come together – *each* member, not just the guys. It's also interesting that they don't seem to notice that a couple of chapters earlier (11:5) Paul affirms women praying and prophesying.

Some scholars think Paul was talking about particular women who needed to stop spreading gossip, disrupting worship by speaking out loud at the wrong moment, or something else very specific to the situation of the Corinthian church. Others think someone other than Paul inserted these words when this letter, written specifically to the Corinthian church, started getting copied and passed around to other churches.

In 1 Timothy 2:12 Paul says women shouldn't teach and should keep silent. Those who point to this verse as evidence that God does not want women to be ordained say that teaching includes preaching. Upon closer reading, however, it seems like this verse is more of a prohibition against a woman usurping authority. Paul is saying that women shouldn't steal authority from the rightfully appointed male leaders, not that they should be forbidden to ever teach (or preach) in church. Anyone who points to this verse as forbidding women ministers really should also deal with the verses before it which say women shouldn't braid their hair, or wear gold or pearls or expensive clothes. Why would one prohibition be so much more important than the other?

Those who say women shouldn't be ministers also point to the qualifications for church leaders listed in 1 Timothy 3, where only male language is used for those church leaders. If only males are mentioned, the thinking goes, then only males can be leaders. Applying that logic to the whole letter, though, means that we have to say that only men will be saved (2:4), only men should pray (2:8), only men should pursue

Notes:

Notes:

righteousness (6:11), and only men with more than one child can be ministers (3:4). The Bible never specifically says to ordain men as ministers either, but most of these people don't seem to have a problem with the church doing that.

Theological Underpinnings

Some Christians are opposed to women ministers from a sincere—but mistaken—belief that the Bible forbids it. Some Christians use the Bible—erroneously—to support what they want to believe: that women aren't supposed to be ministers. When we eliminate the misunderstood scriptural support for a position against women ministers, the most likely basis for this disapproval of women clergy seem to be: 1) believing that being a pastor is man's work and no place for a woman, 2) fear of or discomfort with women in positions of authority, 3) choosing "how we've always done it" over what God is doing, 4) an extreme aversion to any kind of change from what's familiar and comfortable. Whatever the reason for someone being opposed to women in ministry, though, doing so is treating earthly things such as these as more important that Godly things such as scripture and the work of the Holy Spirit in calling persons to ministry. Putting earthly things above Godly things is never wise, or good, or pleasing to God.

Even a quick glance through the Bible to see what the scripture says overall about women in ministry – rather than pulling a couple of verses out of context -- reveals that those persons and denominations who don't believe women should be ministers are misinformed.

Applying the Lesson to Your Own Life

If you believe your congregation is already open to and accepting of women in ministry, you should use this lesson anyway. This lesson will help your students better understand why their own congregation and denomination support women in ministry, and will give them the vocabulary to discuss this matter theologically with peers who attend other churches which teach that women should not be ministers. Also, appearances can be deceiving. Some CP churches seem open to women in ministry, until the matter falls right on their doorstep. And, youth who have been around the church for a while may know that the public or corporate position on the matter differs from privately or personally held views of some members. It would be a shame if one of the girls from your youth group disregarded a call from God because she knew her church family would not approve of her seeking ordination. If you're tempted to disregard this lesson because you disapprove of women in ordained ministry, you need to seriously and carefully reevaluate your connection with the Cumberland Presbyterian Church. Proceeding with this lesson. may very well reveal that the source of your disapproval is not from God at all, but from culture.

If you believe that this lesson is important and necessary... go for it, maybe praying specifically for one of your female students whom you think may be called to pursue ordained ministry.

The Lesson

Get Started (5-10 min)

Opening Activity: Goodies for the Guys

Be sneaky about this: don't treat it like the opening activity, but more as part of your pre-meeting fellowship time.

Announce that Mr. / Mrs. (insert name) stopped by today with some homemade goodies and said, "I made these for all the guys in the youth group." Be careful how you say this: emphasize "all" and not "guys." Distribute the goodies, but only give them to the boys. Have in hand only enough for the boys. Keep the extra goodies hidden away so that your container or plate is empty after all the boys have one. If you end up with a few extra on the serving plate, give some boys two treats until the plate is empty. If you are a male, take one yourself; if not, don't. If you use store-bought treats, use the same story that someone gave them to you to share with the guys in the youth group. It's important that the goodies not come from you.

Hopefully, your students will object immediately. If you need to, though, ham it up a bit by (if you're a guy) chewing right in front of a girl and talking about how good the treat is and how it's too bad she can't have any, or (if you're a girl) by talking about how good the treat looks and how you're so hungry. Ignore the complaints for a bit, but eventually say something like, *But Mr. / Mrs. (insert name) said these are for all the guys*

Leader Tip:

Bullying is the most common form of persecution presented in today's media. A YouTube search will produce several potential videos that you might consider using as your getting started activity. Or you might choose to create your own video or record the Instant Skits for fun.

Leader Tip:

Use the guy/girl difference conversation as a time to affirm that men and women are different. Allow generalizations such as "girls talk about their feelings more than guys do", but note that they are generalizations. Challenge unfounded stereotypes such as "guys are stupid". Let your students respond to one another's comments, but keep it civil.

in the youth group." Play dumb and stick to your position that "guys" means males alone. The goal is for your students, hopefully both male and female, to try to convince you that the goodies were meant for everyone in the group. Resist for a while. You may even want to ask leading questions, though still acting as if you believe the goodies are for the boys alone, something along the lines of: but why would she say "guys" if she meant everybody; or, but guys are more active and need more food don't they; or, girls don't even like these things do they? When your students have presented a good argument, pretend to be convinced, bring out the rest of the goodies and give them to the girls.

If you have a group with a vast majority of girls, go ahead with this activity as written; it may be even more powerful that way. If you happen to have a group of only girls, try this alternative: substitute the word "young people" for "guys" and only give goodies to the youngest third of your students. Your position in the ensuing debate would be that the church member meant the goodies for the younger members of the group because he or she said "young people."

Listen Up (25 min)

Discussion Questions:
- What are some differences between guys and girls?
- What are some things people say men should do, but not women?
- Is there anything God says men should do, but not women?

Tell the following story:
When Walter died, Kay had been his pastor for only a few months. It was a part-time position. Kay lived an hour away and just drove to the church on Sundays and Wednesdays; plus she hadn't been there long, so nobody from the community really knew her. But she was the pastor, so when Walter died, Kay did what pastors do at funerals: she prayed, she read scripture, she preached, she stood beside the grave and prayed some more, and she hugged the family.

After the funeral was over a man approached her. Apparently he had known Walter, but he was not a member of the church

Kay was serving; they had never met.

So this guy walks up to Kay, the pastor, and says, 'I've never seen a church secretary do a funeral before.'

It was easier for this guy to believe that the church had the secretary conduct a funeral than it was for him to even imagine that a woman might possibly be a minister. True story! (The names have been changed.)

Say: *Some denominations ordain women as ministers and some do not. Some of those which do not ordain women claim that they base their refusal to do so on scripture.*

Have someone read 1 Corinthians 14:34.

Discussion Question:
- So, what did Paul really mean?

Allow any answers, but explain that scholars don't really know what Paul meant here. Anyone who says he or he does know is guessing. Draw from the background information to offer possibilities.

Have someone read 1 Timothy 2:12.

Discussion Question:
- Why do you think someone would consider this verse to be more important than others, like the one that says not to eat pork or the one that says to pluck out your eye if it leads you to sin?

Have a student read aloud Galatians 3:27-28.

Say: *In this passage, Paul says that in Christ there is no male or female, no Jew or Greek, no enslaved persons or free persons. This means that once we've made Jesus the most important thing in our lives, all the silly and superficial things people use to stereotype and limit and hold back each other—things like gender expectations—are all thrown out the window by Christ himself.*

Say: *Listen to someof the women the Bible mentions as being in ministry.*

- Miriam is called a prophet and is referred to with equal status as Moses and Aaron, two giants of Judaism (Exodus

Notes:

Notes:

15:20, Micah 6:4).
- Deborah is called a prophet and a judge (2 Kings 4). Judges were those select few Israelites who made decisions about religious law. Legally, they were more important than even the priests. Prophets were people chosen by God to receive messages from God and relay them to God's people.
- Huldah was a prophet. Priests came to her and she proclaimed God's word to them (2 Kings 22:14-20).
- Mary Magdalene and some other women, according to Matthew, Luke, and John, were the first to proclaim (or preach) a resurrected Christ.
- In 1 Corinthians Paul refers to Chloe as the leader of a congregation (1:11), and talks about women praying and prophesying in church (1:15).
- Nympha had a church in her house (Colossians 4:15). In the early days of Christianity, each congregation met in the leader's house.
- Priscilla and her husband Aquilla, instructed Apollos in the faith. Apollos went on to be a strong leader in the early church (Acts 18:24-28).
- Eudia and Syntyche are referred to by Paul as his co-workers (Philippians 4:2-3), putting them on an equal level as himself.
- Phoebe is called a deacon of a particular church (Romans 16:1). The same word translated as "deacon" can be translated as "minister".
- Junia is called an apostle (Romans 16:7).

Say: *It's right there in the Bible—women as ministers.*

Show of Hands

Those who want to find support for keeping women from serving as ministers might not let direct scriptural evidence stop them. They may also use inferences from scripture to support their arguments. By a show of hands, poll your students to see if they've heard either of these arguments:

- Because Jesus called 12 men to be his disciples God only means for men to be pastors.
- Jesus only gave authority to men to preach because just before the resurrected Jesus ascended into heaven he told only the male disciples to go to all the world, baptizing and teaching (Matthew 28:16-20 and Mark 16:15-16).

Say: *If you use that same that logic, then women shouldn't receive Holy Communion either, because Matthew 26:20, Mark 14:17-18, and Luke 22:14 seem to say that only the 12 male disciples were there when Jesus instituted this sacrament. And we'd also have to ignore the clear biblical teaching that the first people the resurrected Jesus told to proclaim his resurrection were women (Matthew 28:10). In Mark 16:7 it was an angel who told the women to proclaim this. In Luke 24:9, they just did it without being told (but the other disciples didn't believe them because they were, after all, just women.)*

The Bible never specifically says to ordain women.
Say: *The Bible never specifically says to ordain men as ministers either, but most of these people don't seem to have a problem with the church doing that.*

Discussion Question:
- What other reasons have you heard given for why woman should not be ministers?

Say: *Whatever the reason for someone being opposed to women in ministry, though, doing so is treating earthly things such as these as more important that Godly things such as scripture and the work of the Holy Spirit in calling persons to ministry. Putting earthly things above Godly things is never wise, or good, or pleasing to God.*

Now What? (12 min)

Daughters
Pass out pens and paper. Use this exercise to allow students to process this lesson more deeply. Tell students to pretend that they are 28 years old and they have just found out that they are going to have a baby girl. Have students write a letter to their future daughter expressing their hopes and dreams for her and her relationship with God. Give them 5-10 minutes to write their letter.

Rhetorical Questions:
- Could you imagine telling your daughter that she couldn't do something?
- Could you tell her she couldn't be a minister?

Leader Tip:

Help your students to understand that from the very beginning of our denomination, Cumberland Presbyterians have believed that in order to understand the Bible most clearly, we can't pull out one verse and base important decisions on what we think that one verse means. Instead, we believe that: "In order to understand God's word spoken in and through the scriptures, persons must have the illumination of God's own Spirit. Moreover, they should study the writings of the Bible in their historical settings, compare scripture with scripture, listen to the witness of the church throughout the centuries, and share insights with others in the covenant community" (*Confession of Faith* 1.07). A verse that seems to say one thing often becomes clearer when we read it from a broader perspective, or after comparing it with other passages.

Notes:

 # Live It (5 min)

Share the following story:
Louisa (loo-EYE-zuh) accepted Christ as her savior when she was 12. Not long after that she felt God calling her to become a preacher. But she didn't think she was qualified to be a preacher, and she'd never even heard of a woman preacher. So she didn't respond to God's call.

Louisa got married when she was 17, secretly hoping that she could convince her husband to become a preacher. She thought God might be satisfied with that and leave her alone. But her husband showed no interest in preaching. At the age of 20, now a mother of two, Louisa decided to read the Bible cover to cover in order to prove to herself that women were not supposed to be ministers. When she was done, instead of being let off the hook, she was more firmly convinced that God does call women to ministry, but she still resisted God's call on her own life.

When one of her children became deathly ill, Louisa told God that if he healed the child, she would take it as a sign that God really did want her to preach. The child recovered and Louisa freaked out. In fact, she made herself sick trying to keep from answering God's call. She knew God was calling her to preach, but she just couldn't figure out how she, a woman, could do that. She tried to make excuses, but God wouldn't listen to them. Finally, after six months of being so sick she couldn't leave her bed, she gave in and told God that she would become a preacher. Her health began to improve and God began to open doors for her to preach.

Preaching her first sermon brought her extreme joy. She was finally doing what God intended her to do. But the joy was short-lived. Many of her friends, and even her own father, rejected her. They'd never heard of a woman preacher either and didn't think it was right. But Louisa stuck with it. She completed her education and was ordained as a minister in 1889.

It was not an easy life for her. She traveled a lot to preach and met a lot of resistance, but ended up preaching hundreds of times a year and leading thousands of people to Christ. Her ordination caused quite a bit of controversy in her denomination, the Cumberland Presbyterian Church, controversy that wasn't officially settled until 1921, and unofficially still isn't settled for some people even today.

The Reverend Louisa Woosley died in 1952 at the age of ninety and after an incredibly successful ministry. She died confident that she had done what was right. She had answered God's call upon her life. True story!

Pass out 'Can Preachers Wear High Heels' and have the girl you've asked to pray the closing prayer do so.

Resources used in creating this lesson: *Cumberland Presbyterian Yearbook for 2011, Shall Woman Preach?* By Louisa Woosley

©2011 Discipleship Ministry Team of the Ministry Council of the Cumberland Presbyterian Church, All Rights Reserved.

Just in Case:

Currently, about 10% of the 900 or so ministers in the Cumberland Presbyterian Church are women (as of mid-2011). However, judging from the number of women preparing for ministry and the number of male ministers approaching retirement age, that percentage will grow significantly in the coming decade.

While most of our presbyteries do not hesitate to receive women as candidates for ministry and help them obtain the necessary education to become a minister, relatively few congregations are willing to call a woman minister as pastor. Therefore many CP ministers who happen to be women end up in other types of ministries such as chaplaincy, Christian education, and counseling. A significant number of such women decide to transfer their ordination to other denominations in which their gifts can be better utilized. Some become so discouraged they drop out of ministry all together, feeling as if they have wasted several years of their lives, and possibly being angry with the church and with God.

Can Preachers Wear High Heels?

Biblical Women in Ministry

Miriam: Referred to as prophet. Listed equally with Moses and Aaron. *Exodus 15:20, Micah 6:4*

Deborah: Prophet and judge of Israel. *2 Kings 4*

Huldah: Prophet; proclaims the word of the Lord to the priests. *2 Kings 22:14-20*

Mary Magdalene: First to preach (proclaim) Jesus resurrected. *Matthew 28:1-11, Luke 24:9-10, John 20:17-18*

Chloe: "Chloe's people" means she is the leader. *1 Corinthians 1:11*

Nympha: The church is in her house, meaning she is the leader. *Colossians 4:15*

Priscilla: Equal with Aquila in proclaiming. Paul calls her a co-worker. *Acts 18:24-28, Rom. 16:3*

Eudia and **Syntyche:** Paul refers to them as co-workers. *Philippians 4:2-3*

Phoebe: Deacon of the church in Cenchreae, deacon = minister/servant. *Romans 16:1*

Junia: "Prominent among the apostles." *Romans 16:7*

Corinthian women: Paul refers to women praying and prophesying. *1 Corinthians 11:5*

Biblical Responses to Objections to Women in Ministry

1 Corinthians 14:34 (*women be silent in church*)
Why so literal with this verse alone? Silence = silence.
Compare to 1 Corinthians 14:28 and 11:5
Specific conditions or later insertion?
Compare to all scriptures above and to Matthew 10:32

1   Timothy 2:12 (*women shouldn't teach*)
This is about *usurping* authority more than teaching
Why so literal with this verse alone? What about 1 Timothy 2:9?
Compare to all scriptures above and Matthew 10:32

1 Timothy 3 (*qualifications of church leaders use only male language*)
Why not apply this same logic to 2:4, 2:8, or 6:11?
What about men with 1 or no children? Remarried widowers?
The Greek for "men" and "man" can easily mean "human" or "humankind"

Additional Responses

Galatians 3:27-28 (NLV) "All of you who have been baptized to show you belong to Christ have become like Christ. God does not see you as a Jew or as a Greek. He does not see you as a person sold to work or as a person free to work. He does not see you as a man or as a woman. You are all one in Christ."

Cumberland Presbyterian *Confession of Faith* 1.07 "In order to understand God's word spoken in and through the scriptures, persons must have the illumination of God's own Spirit. Moreover, they should study the writings of the Bible in their historical settings, compare scripture with scripture, listen to the witness of the church throughout the centuries, and share insights with others in the covenant community."

Women in Ministry—By the Numbers

30,000
The approximate number of verses in the rest of the Bible that are either silent on the matter or affirm women in ministry.

1889
The year the Cumberland Presbyterian Church first ordained a woman as minister of word and sacrament: Louisa Woosley, ordained by Nolin Presbytery in Kentucky. This was only the second ordination of a woman in America.

10
Approximate percentage of CP ministers in 2011 who are women.

3
The approximate number of Bible verses that can be understood to say that women should not be ordained ministers.

1
The number of persons you can make sure stand up for women in ministry.

Oops, We Made a Church!
How the CP Church Was Born
By Andy McClung

Scripture: John 3:14-17

Theme: The birth of the Cumberland Presbyterian Church is an exciting story with dynamic and dedicated characters that every CP should know.

Resource List

- A Taboo board game, if you can get one easily. If not, make your own. To make your own, you'll need index cards, a one-minute timer, and newsprint or a whiteboard on which to keep score. You may also wish to have some kind of buzzer or whistle. You can find the rules online.
- Images from the 1800s
- Descriptions of your city, town, or local area from the earliest time period you can manage (1800s if possible). Your local library probably has a special collection. You may also be able to find general descriptions on the Web.
- Copies of the 'Oops, We Made a Church!' handout for each student

 ## Leader Prep

- Gather illustrations or images of your city, town, or local area as early in the nineteenth century as you can. Many towns were not founded until long after the early 1800s and photography was not in general use in the United States until after the Civil War (1861-1865) but what is important is that you demonstrate to your students how different life in the 1800s was from our modern world. Try to find images that show the size of homes, clothing, tools, slave quarters, medical instruments, or anything else that highlights that difference.
- Find descriptions of your city, town, or local area from as early in the 1800s as you can. Your local library may have a special collection. If your town or area was not settled in the early 1800s you may also be able to find general descriptions on the Web.
- If you have the ability to show a website to your group, bookmark the following: map of the U.S.A. in 1810 at worldmapsonline.com/unitedstates1810.htm, and the birthplace of the Cumberland Presbyterian Church at cumberland.org/hfcpc/birthp.htm.
- On the CP website, grab photos of the replica log cabin at the Birthplace "Shrine."
- Check your church's records to find which students have made a profession of faith and which haven't.
- Pray for your students, thanking God for those who have made professions of faith and seeking the guidance of the Holy Spirit in ministering to those who haven't.

Notes:

 # Leader Insights

Connecting to Your Students
Just as we need to prepare the resources for a lesson, we need to prepare our hearts and minds for the Biblical and theological insights each lesson provides. Familiarize yourself with these insights to help you respond to the discussion questions and activities throughout the lesson. This lesson is a leader insight unto itself. You will want to thoroughly review the history and theology of the Cumberland Presbyterian Church presented below before the lesson.

It's rare for teens to care about history, but some enjoy old family stories. Make this lesson as interesting as possible by being very familiar with the background material. That way, you can tell your students an exciting story instead of reading them boring history. Every Cumberland Presbyterian should know how our denomination came about

Historical Background
In North America around 1800, almost everything west of the Mississippi River was either Spanish territory, wilderness, or occupied by Native Americans. Many places east of the Mississippi were still pretty wild. Kentucky and Tennessee were part of the U.S., but were still claimed by the Native Americans living there. Fighting between white settlers and these indigenous people was common. Settlers didn't go anywhere without a loaded rifle because they feared they might get into skirmishes with Native Americans.

There were 5,308,483 people living in the sixteen United States. Compare that to over 308,000,000 in 2010. New York City was the biggest city by population, with 60,515 people. Compare that to over eight million people in 2010: three million more people live in New York City today than lived in the entire country 200 years ago!

Slavery was common throughout the U.S., not just in the South. Most free people could read and write, and many slave owners taught their slaves how to read and write even though doing so was illegal in many places. Communities, not the government, ran the local school, but only if they could afford to pay a teacher. The average white person only lived to be forty or so, and the average black person didn't live long past twenty. The average woman had seven babies during her life, but only four or five of those babies survived.

There was no air conditioning. Homes were heated by burning wood or coal. There were no telephones, or TVs, or cars, or paved roads, or toilets, or refrigerators, or electricity. There were few stores on the frontier. People made their own clothes, tools, toys, houses, and pretty much everything else they needed. Shoelaces were still a new thing, having been invented only 10 years earlier! Shoes, in fact, were a luxury on the frontier; most people wore moccasin-type shoes made from animal skins. Matches, as we know them, wouldn't be invented for more than twenty years. Bicycles were a new invention and unknown on the frontier. Cokes and other soft drinks were unheard of. Hunting, fishing, and gardening weren't hobbies, but the only way to get food. It took months or even longer for news to travel from place to place. Nothing about life really changed from generation to generation: parents didn't get confused by their kids' new gadgets because the kids had the exact same things their parents and grandparents had.

Your students' closest family members alive at the time probably would have been their great-great-great-great-great-grandparents.

After taking over Ireland in the 1600s, King James I of England relocated many Presbyterian Scots to Ulster, which is where we get the term *Scots-Irish*. (It does not come from an intermarrying of the two ethnicities.) These settlers thrived in their new home, but by the mid-1700s thousands of them were moving out of Ireland each year to escape overcrowding, drought, and conflict with the Roman Catholic Irish. Many of these folk came to the New World and began to push the frontier westward.

Religion was at a low point in America during this time, with ninety percent of people not caring anything about living Christian lives. Some of the families who were carving out homes, farms, and communities from the rugged wilderness, however, also wanted to establish churches. Many of these people were those Presbyterian Scots, so they sent requests back east for ministers to come out to them. Some ministers did, braving the harsh conditions to travel from place to place preaching, or settling somewhere and establishing churches.

In the early 1800s, a revival movement began in Kentucky and swept across the country. Something new developed, large

Notes:

Notes:

gatherings for worship called 'camp meetings.' Hundreds of people would attend these gatherings, driving their wagons, riding their horses, or even walking for days to get to these meetings.

They would then camp there for several more days during the meetings. Sermons lasted for hours and people wept loudly as they confessed their sins and cried out for God's forgiveness. Some people fainted during these services, falling down as if they were dead. Others would lose control of their bodies and jerk around or dance uncontrollably.

As the revival swept the nation, more and more new Christians went back to their homes with a new need: churches to attend on Sundays. The more people there were who wanted to start new churches, the more ministers were needed on the frontier. Unfortunately, there simply were not enough ministers to meet this need. One reason for this among the Presbyterians was the extensive educational requirements for ministers: they had to spend a few years studying at a well-established seminary all the way back in Europe, or on the east coast of the U.S. before they could be ordained and put to work.

The Presbyterian Church on the Frontier

Presbyterian ministers were prominent in leading the revival movement. They became frustrated, though, because the rules of Presbyterianism were holding back this revival movement, which they believed was clearly the work of the Holy Spirit. So, they proposed a different kind of educational model for those preparing for ministry: instead of going off to seminary, they could learn in the field with seminary-educated ministers teaching them in log cabins and on horseback. This way, they said, ministers could be educated and out doing God's work more quickly, which was needed. Most Presbyterians, though, didn't like the revival movement to begin with, so they sure weren't going to agree to anything that helped it along.

The anti-revivalists tried their best to stop the revival movement, but failed. Their problem wasn't just with the new style of worship at the camp meetings, but also with the revival ministers themselves. Many of these revival ministers had begun questioning some of the long-held teachings of the Presbyterian Church.

The primary teaching the revival ministers questioned was the belief that God controlled every tiny detail of what happened in the world, including who was saved through Christ and who wasn't. The Presbyterian belief was that God had decided, long before anyone alive had even been born, who would be saved and who wouldn't. Nobody had any say in whether they were saved or damned. It was all in God's hands and had all been decided long ago. This idea is called predestination, and it's based on an admirably high reverence for God, God's power, and God's authority.

The revival ministers had a high reverence for God as well, but they wanted to have the right to question this teaching of predestination. Because of scriptures such as John 3:16 that seem to say anyone can come to Jesus and be saved, and because of what they'd witnessed at the camp meetings, they had moved away from believing in predestination. They'd come to believe that, with God's help, anyone could accept forgiveness through Jesus Christ and be saved.

Revival Ministers of Cumberland Presbytery

Many of the revival ministers were members of Cumberland Presbytery of the Presbyterian Church. The 'Cumberland' came from the area of Tennessee and Kentucky known as Cumberland Country. When the revival ministers in Cumberland Presbytery refused to stop doing what they believed to be God's work, they were suspended by the Presbyterian Church until they swore fidelity to the Presbyterian rules. The church even dissolved Cumberland Presbytery to keep the revival ministers powerless. Some of the revival ministers gave up and swore fidelity to the rules, choosing to continue ministering according to the Presbyterian rules rather than not be ministering at all. Others kept fighting. In fact, they fought for four years in the church courts, but were never granted the opportunity to fully explain their side of the story.

The Birth of the Cumberland Presbyterian Church

On a cold February morning in 1810, two of the revival ministers set out for Dickson Country, Tennessee. They'd had enough oppression and were determined to do something about it. Their names were Finis Ewing and Samuel King. With them was Ephraim McLean, who was preparing to be a minister. They were going to the home of Samuel McAdow (MAC-uh-doo), another revival minister who had moved away from the fight.

When Ewing and King reached McAdow's home, they explained their idea for a new tactic. They wanted to form a

Notes:

Notes:

new presbytery so they could continue doing ministry and so they would have a voice in the church courts, but they needed three ministers to form a presbytery. Ewing and King asked McAdow to be that third minister.

Legend tells us that McAdow went down to the creek bank and prayed through the cold night. History tells us that, in the morning, he agreed. So, on February 4, 1810, a new presbytery was formed within the Presbyterian Church. They named it Cumberland Presbytery. These men were not at all trying to start a new denomination. They loved the Presbyterian Church and faithfully supported its ministries. They only wanted two things: 1) to be doing ministry in the name of Jesus Christ, and 2) the right to question the teachings of the denomination they were a part of. Despite all their efforts, they had been denied both these things.

Their first act as Cumberland Presbytery was to ordain Ephraim McLean. Then, over the next three years they recruited ministers and laypersons who shared the same questions about Presbyterian theology and practice. They also educated and ordained ministerial candidates. While they were incredibly successful at doing ministry and bringing people to a saving relationship with Jesus Christ, they were completely unsuccessful at being acknowledged as doing legitimate ministry by the Presbyterian Church.

Their numbers grew so rapidly that soon three presbyteries had been formed. With three presbyteries they could form a synod and make a complete break from the Presbyterian Church. Although they had not set out to do so, after a total of seven years of fighting just to be heard, the Cumberland Presbyterians made the break by forming Cumberland Synod in October of 1813, in Sumner County, Tennessee.

Cumberland Synod took two major actions at its first meeting. First, they wrote a brief statement which set forth the four points of Presbyterian theology with which the Cumberland Presbyterians (as they had come to be known) disagreed. Second, they formed a committee to write a new document of belief, called a confession of faith. When Cumberland Synod met again in April of 1814, ten clergy and seventeen laypersons spent four days discussing and adjusting the new Confession of Faith. Finally, it was agreed upon unanimously.

Unquestionably a distinct and separate denomination now,

the Cumberland Presbyterian Church didn't look back, only forward. After all, there was a lot of ministry to be done.

Samuel King, Finis Ewing, and Samuel McAdow had no intention of starting a new denomination when they gathered in Dickson County, Tennessee, on February 4, 1810. They only wanted to bring people into relationship with God through Jesus Christ. The rules of the Presbyterian Church were keeping them from doing that, so they did what they had to. The unintentional result was a new denomination.

This new denomination grew rapidly and spread across the frontier like wildfire. Many states had Cumberland Presbyterian congregations before they were even states officially. In many areas the first Christian worship service was held by Cumberland Presbyterians. The denomination grew to astounding numbers, starting over eighty colleges and schools, thousands of congregations, and extensive mission work to American Indians and several foreign countries.

Then, the Cumberland Presbyterian Church died in 1906 by merging back into the Presbyterian Church. But resurrection followed soon after that death.

Theological Underpinnings

When the Cumberland Presbyterian Church was born, there were two basic ideas about salvation. On one end of the spectrum was Calvinism, which said that God was in absolute control of everything and controlled every tiny detail of what happened in the world, including who was saved and who wasn't. At the other end of the spectrum was Arminianism, which said that it was entirely each person's own choice whether or not to accept Jesus as savior.

The Cumberland Presbyterians developed a whole new theology that falls between these two extremes. Cumberland Presbyterians believe that God, through the work of the Holy Spirit, makes us aware that we are separated from God by sin and calls us into a saving relationship through Christ. God also gives us the faith to respond to that call, but ultimately leaves the choice up to us. We are able to resist God's call and reject salvation if we so choose. If we accept salvation, it's not by our own effort alone, but because God gave us the faith to so choose. So, Cumberland Presbyterians believe humans are saved not by our own faith, but by God's grace. (See *Confession of Faith* 4.08-4.09.)

Just in Case

Native Americans

It is tempting to avoid discussing the conflict between Native Americans and European settlers. Like the slavery issue, it is not a pleasant part of our past. While the indigenous people did not consider the land theirs, they did understandably defend it against the invasion. The U.S. government, for the most part, had secured treaties with representatives from the tribes occupying the land in question. The settlers, then, thought they had every right to move on in. Obviously, the whole thing is far more complicated than that, but as in most such conflicts, there was some blame to be placed on all parties involved.

Leader Tip:

Refer to Confession of Faith 4.08-4.09 for more scriptural support of our beliefs about salvation.

Applying the Lesson to Your Own Life

Do you tend to stick to the familiar or do you prefer to branch out into new things? Does your answer to that question apply to all things: food, recreation, authors, vacation spots, friends, and theological beliefs? If not, in what area are you most likely to try something new? In what area are you most likely to stick with the familar?

Which side would you have been on in the debate that led to the birth of the CP Church, the side that wanted everything to stay as it had been for years or the side that was excited about something new God was doing? How long has it been since God did something new in your life? In your congregation? If it's been a while, why do you think that is? Is it hasn't, how do you know the new thing is from God?
CPs call John 3:16 "the gospel in miniature." If you only had one minute to tell someone about Jesus, do you think quoting John 3:16 would be sufficient? Why or why not?

The Lesson

Get Started (10-15 min)

Taboo

Divide into two teams and play a game of Taboo. If you're not familiar with this game, it's a word guessing game in which a player tries to get his or her teammates to say a certain word without saying that word itself or any of five other specified words (which are usually the most obvious clues). The forbidden words are "taboo," as are hand gestures, rhyming, and making sound effects. Example: Tony draws the card that says "watch." He has one minute to get his team to say the word "watch," but he may not say the words: look, time, wears, wrist, or TV. One person from the other team (or an impartial judge) monitors the clue-giver and buzzes him or her if a taboo word is said. The goal is for each team to guess as many words as possible in the allotted time for their turn. Limit the game to ten minutes or so.

You can easily find a Taboo game or you can make your own. In fact, it may be fun to make your own using people and things around your church. Example: your senior pastor, with the taboo words being descriptive words such as "bald," "preacher," and the names of his family members.

Congratulate the winning team by saying, *"You did a great job of getting done what you needed to get done, even though the rules really limited you."*

 ## Listen Up (25 min)

Discussion Question:
- What do you think life was like in the early 1800s?

Show the 1810 map of the United States on your computer.

Share the images and/or descriptions from your area, if you were able to find any.

Discussion Question:
- If you were to somehow go back to 1800 to live, what modern convenience would you miss the most?

Share information with your students from the Historical Background section to set the tone of what was happening in America in the early 1800s.

Discussion Question:
- Why do you think religion was at a low point in the early 1800s in the U.S.?

Say: *Likely causes were that many immigrants had come from religiously oppressive places, fully focusing on surviving day-to-day leaves little time or energy for anything else, and the solitude of frontier life meant no church or faith community.*

Discussion Question:
- Is it ever okay to break or ignore the rules?
- If so, when?

Share with your students, information from The Presbyterian Church on the Frontier section found in the Leader Insights.

Have someone read aloud John 3:14-17.

Just in Case
Church Government

The word "Presbyterian" refers to a form of church government, not any particular doctrine. There are three basic forms of church government: 1) Episcopal, which has bishops who oversee the church and appoint pastors (Lutheran, United Methodist, Christian Methodist Episcopal); 2) congregational, in which each congregation fends for itself, calls its own pastor, ordains whomever it wishes, and disciplines its own members (Baptist, Disciples of Christ, independent); and 3) Presbyterian. In the Presbyterian system, no congregation is ever alone because all congregations of the same denomination are connected. Each congregation elects persons, called elders, to run their church and also to work with the ministers and elders from a larger area to oversee all the churches in that area. This group is called "presbytery." Overseeing the presbyteries are synods, and overseeing the whole denomination is a General Assembly, both of which are made up of representatives elected by each presbytery. Each congregation calls its own pastor, but the presbytery must approve the relationship before it is official.

Notes:

Discussion Questions:
- Do you think God controls every tiny detail of what happens in the world?
- On what do you base this belief?
- If you think God does control every tiny detail, does that include who is saved and who isn't?
- If you don't think God controls every tiny detail, what causes stuff—good or bad—to happen?

Say: When some ministers from Cumberland Presbytery of the Presbyterian Church refused to stop doing what they believed to be God's work, they were suspended by the Presbyterian Church until they swore that they agreed with the Presbyterian rules. Some of them agreed, but some kept fighting. They fought for four years in the church courts, but were never granted the opportunity to fully explain their side of the story.

On a cold February morning in 1810, two of the revival ministers set out for Dickson Country, Tennessee. They'd had enough oppression and were determined to do something about it. Their names were Finis Ewing and Samuel King. With them was Ephraim McLean, who was preparing to be a minister. They were going to the home of Samuel McAdow (MAC-uh-doo), another revival minister who had moved away from the fight.

Show your students the photos of the replica log cabin at the Birthplace "Shrine."

When Ewing and King reached McAdow's home, they explained that they wanted to form a new presbytery so they could continue doing ministry and so they would have a voice in the church courts, but they needed three ministers to form a presbytery. Ewing and King asked McAdow to be that third minister.

Legend tells us that McAdow went down to the creek bank and prayed through the cold night. History tells us that, in the morning, he agreed. So, on February 4, 1810, a new presbytery was formed within the Presbyterian Church. They named it Cumberland Presbytery. These men were not at all trying to start a new denomination. They loved the Presbyterian Church and faithfully supported its ministries. They only wanted two things: 1) to be doing ministry in the name of Jesus Christ, and 2) the right to question the teachings of the denomination they were a part of. Despite all their efforts, they had been denied both these things.

Their first act as Cumberland Presbytery was to ordain Ephraim McLean. Then, over the next three years they recruited ministers and laypersons who shared the same questions about Presbyterian theology and practice. They also educated and ordained ministerial candidates. While they were incredibly successful at doing ministry and bringing people to a saving relationship with Jesus Christ, they were completely unsuccessful at being acknowledged as doing legitimate ministry by the Presbyterian Church.

Their numbers grew so rapidly that soon three presbyteries had been formed. With three presbyteries they could form a synod and make a complete break from the Presbyterian Church. Although they had not set out to do so, after a total of seven years of fighting just to be heard, the Cumberland Presbyterians made the break by forming Cumberland Synod in October of 1813, in Sumner County, Tennessee.

Cumberland Synod wrote a new Confession of Faith and adopted it in April of 1814. This unquestionably made them a distinct and separate denomination, the Cumberland Presbyterian Church.

Samuel King, Finis Ewing, and Samuel McAdow had no intention of starting a new denomination when they gathered in Dickson County, Tennessee, on February 4, 1810. They only wanted to bring people into relationship with God through Jesus Christ. The rules of the Presbyterian Church were keeping them from doing that, so they did what they had to. The unintentional result was a new denomination.

Now What? (7-10 min)

What We Believe

Say: *When the Cumberland Presbyterian Church was born, there were two basic ideas about salvation. On one end of the spectrum was Calvinism, which said that God controlled every tiny detail of what happened in the world, including who was saved and who wasn't. At the other end of the spectrum was Arminianism, which said that it was entirely each person's*

Leader Tip:

The CP Church today:
At the end of 2010, the Cumberland Presbyterian Church had 711 congregations, 913 ministers, and 76,158 members. We have a presence (either congregations or mission sites) in twenty-two states of the U.S.A. and in twelve other countries.

Notes:

own choice whether or not to accept Jesus as savior.

The Cumberland Presbyterians developed a whole new theology that falls between these two extremes. Cumberland Presbyterians believe that God, through the work of the Holy Spirit, makes us aware that we are separated from God by sin and calls us into a saving relationship through Christ. God also gives us the faith to respond to that call, but ultimately leaves the choice up to us. If we accept salvation, it's not by our own effort alone, but because God gave us the faith to so choose. So, Cumberland Presbyterians believe humans are saved not by our own faith, but by God's grace.

Save time to allow students who have made a profession of faith to talk about it, sharing their experiences. Draw attention to the parts of their stories that correspond with the Cumberland Presbyterian idea of God calling us first, and then giving us the faith to respond to that call. Note that your students may not use that kind of language. Be sure to thank everyone who shares a story.

 ## Live It (5 min)

Have the group join in a circle for the closing prayer.

Pray: *Thank you, God for the brave men and women of the past who started the Cumberland Presbyterian Church. Thank you for its many years of faithful ministry. Thank you for its groundbreaking theology. And please continue to bless the many ministries of this denomination around the world. We pray now that you would call anyone among this group who has not yet made Christ the most important thing in his or her life. Cal them, and give them the faith to respond. Amen.*

Resources used in creating this lesson: *A People Called Cumberland Presbyterians* by Ben Barrus and others, *Confession of Faith, History of the Cumberland Presbyterian Church* by B.W. McDonnold, *Studies in Cumberland Presbyterian History* by Thomas Campbell, the U.S. Census Bureau, *2011 Yearbook of the Cumberland Presbyterian Church*

©2011 Discipleship Ministry Team of the Ministry Council of the Cumberland Presbyterian Church, All Rights Reserved.

OOPS!
We Made a Church!

The Cumberland Presbyterian Church was born in Dickson County, Tennessee, on February 4, 1810.

Samuel King (1775-1842) was born in North Carolina and moved to Tennessee while a child. A poor farmer, he had a compulsion to share Jesus with the unsaved. In 1804 he became a Presbyterian minister and soon felt called to do more for God that the strictures of the Presbyterian Church would allow. Reportedly, his incredible power in the pulpit (despite his missing front teeth) came from his being a devout man of prayer. King's ministry led to the first indigenous ministers among the Choctaw. He died in Missouri from a fever.

Samuel McAdow (1760-1844) was born in North Carolina. His long-held feeling of a call to the ministry was sidetracked for a time by the responsibilities of farm and family. After leaving the farm and losing his wife, he began to preach full time. He believed in theological education for ministers, but also believed that such an education was worthless without the baptism of the Holy Spirit. After extensive traveling and preaching he settled in Tennessee, where, against medical advice, he continued to preach. It was at his "old log house" that the CP Church was born. He died in Illinois, the fame of his name, and home, a sharp contrast to the unassuming life he led.

Finis Ewing (1773-1841) was born in Virginia, the twelfth and last child of his parents. ("Finis" means "the end".) Though he grew up going to church he did not truly become a Christian until he was an adult. He found himself occasionally preaching, and the effectiveness of his sermons led him to recognize the call to ministry. Ewing strongly advocated and supported education for ministers throughout his life and even in his will. Ewing was a slave owner, but became convicted that slavery was inconsistent with a Christian life, saying "traffic in human flesh and human souls" is evil. He freed his slaves upon his death in Missouri.

You and the CP Church!

◆Ewing, King, and McAdow didn't mean to start a new denomination. Have you ever accidentally done something that turned out well? Journal about your experience or discuss it with your family at the dinner table. Does it give you any insights into how our founders might have felt?

◆Look at what your church does. Ask your parents, youth leader, elders, or the pastor: What does your church do to share Christ with others? How often is the story about the birth of our denomination told? Are there plans for a special celebration of the C.P. Church's birthday on the Sunday closest to February 4 next year?

◆This week, ask three of your classmates, neighbors, teammates, or co-workers if they go to church. If they do, ask what denomination they belong to, how it started, what are some of its basic beliefs. If they don't, explain the basic belief of C.P. Church (God calls us to salvation through Christ and gives us the faith to respond to that call) and invite them to come to church with you next Sunday.

Are Christians Cannibals?
A Look at Holy Communion

By Andy McClung

Scripture: Matthew 26:26-29

Theme: The celebration of Holy Communion is the central act of Christian worship. This lesson familiarizes students with the Cumberland Presbyterian beliefs about this sacrament.

Resource List

- Ingredients and other stuff for making bread (See recipe on next page.)
- Grape juice and cup(s) for communion
- Copies of 'Are Christians Cannibals?' handout for each student

Leader Prep

- Ask someone who can bake to help with this lesson.
- Ask your church's pastor to serve communion at the end of this lesson
- Plan to sing a communion hymn—to CD, live music, or *a capella*—to close this lesson.
- Pray for God to be active in the lives of your students leading up to this lesson, for yourself as you lead this lesson, and especially for those youth who have not yet made a profession of faith.

Leader Insights

Connecting to Your Students

Just as we need to prepare the resources for a lesson, we need to prepare our hearts and minds for the Biblical and theological insights each lesson provides. Familiarize yourself with these insights to help you respond to the discussion questions and activities throughout the lesson. This lesson is a leader insight unto itself. Therefore, take the time to read through the lesson and learn all about communion and the Cumberland Presbyterian understanding of communion.

Youth who have grown up in church may or may not know what communion is all about, but they certainly know it's something different, something special. Youth who are new to church may have an even greater understanding of this because worship practices are still new to them. They haven't

Notes:

had time for familiarity to breed boredom. For most youth, a special communion service just for them is more powerful than feeling like a guest in the grown up service. Be sure to emphasize that Jesus did what he did for each and every one of your students.

Explaining the Lesson
Most Protestant denominations recognize two sacraments: baptism and Holy Communion. Communion is also called The Lord's Supper and The Eucharist.

A sacrament is a vehicle for God's grace. That is, an officially recognized action through which God's grace always comes to those engaging in the action. Yes, God is always present in the sacrament of Holy Communion, even when we don't recognize that presence.

Because we make such a big deal about communion in church, you might think that a lot of the Bible is dedicated to the topic. But really, its origin is detailed in just four places: Matthew 26:26-29, Mark 14:22-26, Luke 22:17-20, and 1 Corinthians 11:23-28, and these are all really just retellings of the same event. Communion is also mentioned, or at least referred to, in a few other passages such as 1 Corinthians 10:16-17, 11:20-22, 27-32. It may seem weird that something so briefly mentioned in the Bible has led to such a widely-practiced ritual, but then again most Christian traditions that we're familiar with actually began in the early church or even later, after the biblical writings were completed.

Communion is a big deal for Christians because Jesus himself started it... and because of the whole "vehicle of God's grace" thing. Additionally, Jesus linked communion to one of the most important holy days in Judaism—the earliest Christians were Jewish—making communion a big deal for them. They passed it along to us. Passover was when the Jewish people remembered that God had freed their ancestors from generations of slavery in Egypt and then led them through the wilderness into their own land, the place God had promised them long before.

Some people called the early Christians cannibals. This misunderstanding arose because for the first few centuries after Jesus' death and resurrection it was illegal to be a Christian.

Christians were thrown in prison, or thrown to the lions in the

Roman coliseum. This persecution lasted from just after the resurrection up until the year A.D. 313. At least, that's when the official, legal persecution ended. Christians are still persecuted in many places in the world today, many of them persecuted to the point of death.

Back when all Christians had to meet and worship in secret to keep from being arrested, word leaked out that they were practicing some kind of weird ritual that involved eating somebody's flesh and drinking somebody's blood. So in some places, Christians were accused of being cannibals. They weren't cannibals, of course, but this was a fairly common misunderstanding and accusation.

Different Christians believe different things about communion. Some say you have to use bread and real wine, others say bread and grape juice, which is basically unfermented wine, are okay. Cumberland Presbyterians say that it has to be juice from grapes, but each congregation can choose between real wine or grape juice. Most choose grape juice.

The focus of communion is different for different Christians as well. Some focus on **remembering** the sacrifice Jesus made to make our salvation possible, the sacrifice of his flesh and blood. Others focus on this sacrament as an act of **thanksgiving** that celebrates God's grace given to us through Jesus. Others focus on the idea that when we partake in this sacrament, we are **supernaturally united** with (or in communion with) the risen Christ and with all other Christians—past, present, and future—who also recognize and partake in it. Limiting ourselves to just one focus, though, doesn't make much sense. Why not strive to get as much as possible out of this God-given sacrament?

Even with all these differences, communion is perhaps the most significant factor which unites all Christians. Details of belief and practice differ between denominations, but all Christians agree that Jesus gave us communion, that participating in this sacrament provides spiritual nourishment, and that God's grace comes through this action when we do it.

CP Beliefs about Communion
Cumberland Presbyterians believe and practice that only ordained ministers can preside at a communion service. This may not seem fair, but this sacrament is so important, it really

Notes:

needs to be done properly. Ideally, the minister asks God's blessings on the bread and wine, and then gives them to the elders, who then give them to the congregation. Under special circumstances an elder from a particular congregation may be given permission to preside over a communion service at his or her church.

Officially, Cumberland Presbyterians recognize all three focuses mentioned above: remembering, celebrating, and Christ's spirit being among us. Each congregation, though, might emphasize one of these more than the other two.

Who may receive communion can be a touchy question for some. Officially, to receive communion, a person should have already made a public profession of faith in Jesus Christ. This does not mean, however, that God's grace is absent from the sacrament when it's received by someone who has not yet made such a profession.

Most congregations leave the decision to the individual, or in the case of children, to their parents.

Cumberland Presbyterians never say that a person has to be Cumberland Presbyterian, or believe exactly like us, or be free of sin, or meet any other requirement to receive communion. Like Jesus, we try to be more inclusive than exclusive.

While communion usually comes near the end of the worship service, it should never be treated or considered as something just added on to worship. This sacrament is a central part of corporate worship. On Sundays that communion is celebrated, all other parts of the worship service might even make allusions to communion.

Theological Underpinnings

There are three different ideas held by Christians about what happens to the bread and the wine during the celebration of Holy Communion.
1. The bread and wine actually become the body and blood of Christ.
2. The bread and wine don't exactly become the body and blood of Christ, but neither do they just remain bread and wine. They become something different from what they were.
3. The bread and wine never become anything other than bread and wine. As we celebrate communion using these elements, the spirit of Christ is among us.

Cumberland Presbyterians fall into this last group, but still treat the bread and wine with respect after it has been consecrated for use in communion.

By making the bread for communion, students will gain a stronger sense of God taking common things and making them sacred. By studying the meaning behind communion, the sacrament will become for them more than just a ritual. By celebrating communion, they will receive the grace of God.

Pay careful attention throughout this lesson to see what your students have come to understand about communion from church. If they have a good grasp on it, congratulate the elders and pastor. If your students do not seem to have a good grasp on the meaning and importance of communion, convey this to the church session as well.

Applying the Lesson to Your Own Life
What is your earliest memory of communion? Did you ever have any ideas about communion that you later realized were inaccurate, or even silly?

Do you look forward to celebrating communion in worship? Can you remember a particular communion service that was especially meaningful? What made it so special?

Does your church treat communion as this sacrament deserves? If so, be sure to thank the elders and pastor. If not, consider asking the church session to make changes that treat communion with the specialness and holiness it merits.

The Lesson

Get Started (15-20 min)

Making Bread

Find someone in your church who is a good baker and explain that you would like him or her to come spend twenty minutes or so helping the youth make some kind of bread that will be ready to eat at the end of the meeting. A regular loaf of bread takes too long to make, so consider asking your baker about

Notes:

Notes:

biscuits, breadsticks, or something else that doesn't take as long. Your baker may offer to simply bake something for the group, but the goal is for your students to take part in making this bread.

Can't find a baker? No problem. Find any adult help and . follow this recipe to make twelve to eighteen breadsticks. Make sure each youth hand a chance to help.

1 cup warm water
3 tablespoons brown sugar
1 teaspoon salt
1/4 cup oil
3 cups bread flour or all purpose flour
Extra flour
2 1/2 teaspoons yeast
Rolling pin
Cookie sheet
Non-stick cooking spray

Preheat the oven to 375°. Mix brown sugar, salt, flour, and yeast. Stir in the water. Stir in the oil. Sprinkle some extra flour on a hard, flat surface and have students take turns kneading the dough for a total of about three minutes. Roll out the dough (use more flour to reduce sticking) into a 10 by 12 inch rectangle. Cut into strips 3/4 inch wide. Give each strip a twist or two and place them all on a slightly greased pan, at least an inch apart. Set aside the dough for 20 to 30 minutes while you continue the lesson. Bake for 10 to 15 minutes at 375°.

 ## Listen Up (25 min)

Learning about Holy Communion

Say: *A sacrament is a vehicle for God's grace. That is, an officially recognized action through which God's grace always comes to those engaging in the action. Most Protestant denominations recognize two sacraments: baptism and Holy Communion. Next weel we'll talk about baptism. This week we're focusing on communion.*

Briefly explain communion's roots in Judaism.

Discussion Question:
- Why do you think early Christians were accused of being cannibals?

Allow answers, and then explain how being Christian was illegal, Christians met and worshiped and celebrated communion in secret, thus giving rise to rumors and misinformation.

Discussion Question:
- What do you think happens in communion -- not the mechanics of the service, but what does God do?

Allow answers, and thank students who venture answers. Some students may offer testimony on what communion means to them. Be careful not to discount anyone's personal experience.

Explain the three different ideas about what happens to the bread and wine, and affirm the CP belief on this.

Say: *Communion may be most significant thing that unites all Christians. All Christians agree that Jesus gave us communion, that participating in this sacrament provides spiritual nourishment, and that God's grace comes through this action when we do it.*

Discussion Question:
- Why do you think the rule in the Cumberland Presbyterian Church is that only ordained ministers can preside at a communion service (and, under special circumstances, an elder)?

If necessary, explain that this sacramentis so important, it really needs to be done right. And that takes education and training.

Say: *Cumberland Presbyterians never say that a person has to be Cumberland Presbyterian, or believe exactly like us, or be free of sin, or meet any other requirement to receive communion. Like Jesus, we try to be more inclusive than exclusive.*

Explain the different parts of a communion service. Be aware that services can look different for different occasions and in different settings, but for Cumberland Presbyterians a few things must be included and some things are usually included:

Notes:

> **Leader Tip:**
>
> When explaining those things to be included in a communion service, create a poster or write them on a dry erase board as a reference point while discussing each.

- *Invitation to the Table.* This is when the minister invites those who have entrusted their lives to Christ to partake in this sacrament.
- *Words of Institution.* This is reading or retelling the story of Jesus instituting, or inventing, this sacrament.
- *Prayer of Thanksgiving.* This is a prayer that gives thanks to God for the life, death, and resurrection of Jesus Christ. This prayer may also ask God to bring the congregation into communion with the spirit of the risen Christ during the celebration of this sacrament.
- *Prayer of Consecration.* There is usually another prayer which asks the Holy Spirit to consecrate the bread and the wine, setting them aside from all ordinary use for this sacred use.
- *Partaking.* The bread is always given and eaten first, in keeping with the scripture story.
- *A song, hymn, charge, prayer, or blessing* usually concludes this part of the worship service.

If your church only serves communion one way, explain the different ways of doing it. Have a student summarize these on newsprint or a whiteboard as you explain.

- *Worshipers can sit in the pew, have the bread and wine brought to them, and then pass these elements down the row. This reflects our being served as Christ served us in his sacrifice.*
- *Worshipers can come forward, making the journey to the communion table. This reflects the spiritual journey we must take to approach God through Christ. Once at the communion table, worshipers might be invited to kneel and pray before receiving the elements or they might receive the elements and return to their seats to pray.*
- *The pastor might partake first, and then serve the elders, who then serve the people. This is a way to say, "Because this grace has been given to me, I can now offer it to you."*
- *The pastor and elders might serve the congregation first, waiting until last to partake of the bread and wine for themselves. This is a way to say, "Serving others is more important than receiving for yourself."*
- *The bread may be a loaf from which each worshiper takes a piece, or it may be individual bits of bread.*
- *The wine may be in individual cups or it may be in a common cup from which everyone drinks.*
- *Intinction, dipping the bread into the cup and then eating bread and wine together, is growing in popularity. This*

> **Leader Tip:**
>
> If your youth seem particularly interested in any of the methods of serving communion which your church does not employ, invite your students to speak to the church session about trying a different method in the near future

method is more practical than theological. There is no special theological significance to, or biblical support for, doing it this way.
- *Worshipers might eat and drink immediately upon receiving the bread and wine, or they might hold the elements until everyone's been served and then eat and drink together. The first reminds us that we must each make a decision for Christ while the second reminds us that we are one community of faith.*
- *An uncommon, but potentially meaningful, method is for all worshipers to eat the bread together, symbolizing that they are one "body" or community of faith and that the church is the "Body of Christ" in the world today; then they can each drink the cup as individuals, symbolizing that Christ's blood was shed for each of them as an individual and that each person has to accept God's gift of forgiveness through Jesus.*
-

Discussion Question:
- What do you think of these different ways?
- Are any new to you?
- What is your favorite way of receiving communion?

Now What? (10 min)

Communion Service

Depending on the size of your group, plan for about 10-12 minutes for this Communion Service. To start, ask someone to read aloud Matthew 26:26-29. Then (unless you are an ordained CP minister, or are an ordained minister from another denomination with presbyterial approval to preside over communion in this church) have the pastor lead the group in a communion service. Encourage him or her not to preach, but to allow the sacrament itself to be the sole focus of this time.

Use the bread the group made earlier as the bread for communion. Arrange things so that communion is the last thing to happen in the meeting and that the group parts ways with a worshipful attitude.

Just in Case:

If a student asks about the frequency of celebrating communion, especially in comparison with other denominations, explain that some congregations celebrate Holy Communion every Sunday, some monthly, and others less frequently. Each Cumberland Presbyterian congregation sets its own schedule for how often they celebrate, but the Confession of Faith does say it should be celebrated regularly.

Just in Case:

If you have students of other denominations visiting, assure them that they are welcome to participate in the communion service. It may be, however, that this student's denomination frowns upon their members receiving communion from another denomination's minister. If so, or if the student just doesn't know what to do, don't push. Explain that in the Cumberland Presbyterian Church, all believers are welcome to partake, and then let them make up their own minds.

Notes:

 # Live It (5 min.)

Conclude the worship service by singing a communion hymn together, such as "Let us Break Bread Together."

Ask the pastor to allow you to pray the prayer after communion.

Prayer: *Thank you, God, for nourishing us with this sacrament. Now we ask that you send us out from this place to nourish the world with your love, compassion, grace, and mercy. This we pray in the name of Jesus Christ, whose spirit is among us now. Amen*

Distribute the 'Are Christians Cannibals?' handouts as students leave.

Resources used in creating this lesson: food.com recipes, *Confession of Faith*.

©2011 Discipleship Ministry Team of the Ministry Council of the Cumberland Presbyterian Church, All Rights Reserved.

Are Christians Cannibals?

Holy Communion, The Lord's Supper, The Eucharist: 3 names—1 Sacrament

Jesus instituted the sacrament of Communion:

Matthew 26:26-29 (New Living Translation), "As they were eating, Jesus took some bread and blessed it. Then he broke it in pieces and gave it to the disciples, saying, 'Take this and eat it, for this is my body.' And he took a cup of wine and gave thanks to God for it. He gave it to them and said, 'Each of you drink from it, for this is my blood, which confirms the covenant between God and his people. It is poured out as a sacrifice to forgive the sins of many. Mark my words—I will not drink wine again until the day I drink it new with you in my Father's Kingdom.'"

Reflect on Communion this week:
1. Did I feel the presence of Christ as we celebrated communion at the youth meeting? If so, share your experience with someone. If not, reflect further: Was it that Christ wasn't there, or was it that I just didn't feel him? Why wouldn't I feel him if he was there?
2. When we have communion in Sunday morning church, what's my favorite part? Why is that my favorite?
3. Which is more important to me: remembering Jesus' sacrifice for me, celebrating God's gift of forgiveness made possible through Jesus' death, or experiencing the spirit of the risen Christ?
4. In what movies, T.V. shows, books, music videos, and song lyrics have I see subtle communion images and themes recently (such as people sharing a loaf of bread or a cup)?
5. How can I be the "body of Christ" this week?

Baby Showers: Baptism in the C.P. Church

By Andy McClung

Scripture: Matthew 3:13-17

Theme: The sacrament of baptism is a vital part of the Christian life. This lesson familiarizes students with what Cumberland Presbyterians believe about this sacrament.

Resource List

- Large garbage bags with head and arm holes cut, enough for half of your group
- Water squirters of any sort, enough for half your group (it's best if these all held the same amount of water)
- Garden hose with a nozzle for Opening Activity Outdoor Option
- Mop(s) for Opening Activity Indoor Option
- Bath towels, enough for half your group
- Two big beach towels
- Salty and/or dry snacks
- Enough identical cups for half your students
- A measuring cup at least equal in size to the identical cups
- Pitchers of ice water and enough drinking cups for all, or water bottles for all
- Blindfold

Resource List continues next page.

Leader Prep

- You'll need a large outdoor area enough where lots of water hitting the ground is no problem, or you'll need an inside space where you can spread bath towels on the floor to absorb splashed water.
- Disable water fountains and drink machines, and do whatever else is necessary to insure that students do not have access to drinks during the lesson.
- Hide your pitchers of water or water bottles somewhere that the youth will not go during the lesson.
- Check church records and/or phone parents to find out who among your students has been baptized and who has not.
- Set up the tabletop fountain somewhere in your meeting space. Make it out of the way, but not hidden. Keep it running throughout the meeting.
- Pray, thanking God for water and the gift of baptism. Ask God for guidance, clarity, and patience as you lead this lesson. Pray also for any students who have not yet made a profession of faith.

Leader Insights

Connecting to Your Students

Just as we need to prepare the resources for a lesson, we need to prepare our hearts and minds for the Biblical and theological insights each lesson provides. Familiarize yourself with these insights to help you respond to the discussion

161

Resource List

- Pads or sheets of paper, one for every two or three students
- Pens, one for every two or three students
- A tabletop decorative fountain, preferably one in which the water makes some noise
- A copy of 'Baby Showers: Baptism in the CP Church' for each student

questions and activities throughout the lesson. This lesson is a leader insight unto itself. Therefore, take the time to read through the lesson and learn all about baptism and the Cumberland Presbyterian understanding of baptism.

Your students may have a wide variety of ideas and experiences about baptism. Some of these ideas may be strongly held. Some of these ideas may be in conflict with Cumberland Presbyterian doctrine that you find in this lesson and in the Confession of Faith. As you lead this lesson, take care not to chastise anyone for their ideas about baptism, but neither should you discount orthodox CP doctrine just to lessen anyone's discomfort.

Explaining the Lesson

Most Protestant denominations recognize two sacraments: baptism and Holy Communion. A sacrament is a vehicle for God's grace. That is, an officially recognized action through which God's grace always comes to those engaging in the action. So, most Christians believe that God is always present in the sacrament of baptism.

We make a pretty big deal out of baptism in church, and rightly so. It's mentioned a lot in the Bible.

Baptism did not start as a Christian thing, but a Jewish thing. Jesus, however, gave baptism a Christian meaning when he received it. The earliest Christians picked up on its importance and passed it along through the centuries to today.

Matthew, Mark, and Luke all record the story of Jesus' baptism by John the Baptizer at the Jordan River. John, the gospel writer, alludes to it as well.

John the Baptizer said he was baptizing people as a sign of their repentance, so this baptism represented their turning away from their sins and turning toward God. Jesus, however, was without sin. He had nothing to repent of. He had no sin to turn from. He was already turned toward God. Why Jesus sought baptism, then, is one of those mysteries of the faith. Maybe it was to show us that baptism is more about what God does than what we do. By asking John to baptize him, Jesus pushed aside all arguments about who was more important, who had power over whom, and instead drew attention to what's most important in baptism: not the one doing the baptizing or even the one receiving the baptism, but God.

Another possibility is that Jesus received baptism to affirm that he was God's son and to set the standard that when we receive baptism God claims us as his children.

In the Old Testament, those who worshiped God and tried to live lives pleasing to God had a religious ritual called circumcision. This ritual was practiced on boys when they were eight days old and symbolized the child belonging to God's people.

Some students may have an inaccurate idea of what circumcision is. Unfortunately, saying something like, "Does everybody know what circumcision is?" does not help. So, to keep anyone from having to be embarrassed (except possibly you, dedicated teacher), consider explaining circumcision: When a baby boy is born he has a sheath of skin, called the foreskin, which covers the tip of his penis. Circumcision is the cutting away of that foreskin, but nothing else. If not cut away, the foreskin remains, growing as the rest of the body grows. Jewish people probably didn't invent circumcision, but they did practice it as a religious act. Today, outside of Judaism, parents choose whether or not to have their infant boys circumcised for a variety of reasons.

In the New Testament, after Jesus' death and resurrection, non-Jewish people started joining the the church. Some of the men—not at all surprisingly—didn't want to be circumcised to join this new religion. And women, whom Jesus had always included, were completely excluded by the old ritual of circumcision. In Acts 15, the leaders of the church decided to expand on what Jesus had started when he presented himself to John for baptism. They made baptism, rather than circumcision, the sign of being a member of God's family.

Forms of Baptism
All Christian denominations agree that baptism is important, but they're not all in agreement about the details. In fact, they're not even close to being in agreement.

There are two ways of practicing baptism.
1. To baptize a person when he or she makes a decision to entrust his or her life to Jesus. Let's call this 'believer baptism.'
2. The other way is to baptize babies of Christian parents as a sign of those babies being part of God's family. Let's call this 'infant baptism'.

Rainstorm Brainstorm

Divide the group into pairs or groups of 4-6. Give each group a sheet of paper and a pen. Say something like, *"There's just been a rainstorm and you collected a giant bucket full of water. Write down as many things as you can think of that you could do with that water. Be creative in your thinking. Be specific in your answers. You have three minutes. Go."*

When time is up, choose one team to read each item on their list. The other teams are to speak up if they have the same item on their lists. Answers given by more than one team are marked through on all lists. The only answers that count are those that no other team came up with. (Example: "washing a car," "washing socks," and "washing an apple" count as three answers, none of which is an exact match for "washing stuff.")

When all lists have been read and you're sure all repeated (or non-unique) answers have been marked through on every list, have each team count their remaining, unique, answers. The team with the most unique answers wins.

Secret Bonus: any answer dealing with baptism is worth five points!

> **Leader Tip:**
>
> It's likely that some of your students will know that they were baptized, and some will not. Some may respond by saying they think they were, but they don't remember it because they were babies.
>
> One of the goals of this lesson should be for students to talk with their parents and learn more about when they were baptized and consider being baptized if they have not been.

The temptation is to say that baptism is baptism, and it means the same thing regardless of the age at which it's done. That, however, is not true at all. For most, believer baptism symbolizes that a person has decided to accept God's gift of forgiveness made possible through Jesus Christ.

On the other hand, infant baptism, for most, symbolizes God claiming a child as God's own and promising someday to call that child to establish a saving relationship through Christ and lead a Christ-like life. See the difference? One starts with the person's decision and the other starts with God's decision.

Christians practice two very different methods of baptism: some completely immerse the person being baptized in water, and some pour water over the recipient's head. Some denominations that hold a believer-only idea of baptism immerse, some pour, and some do either, but most baby baptizing denominations don't immerse infants!

Immersing someone being baptized symbolizes that person dying to his or her old self and rising again with the resurrected Christ. Pouring water on the recipient's head symbolizes the Holy Spirit pouring over his or her life. Both methods indicate that the baptized person is now marked by God. Both methods can be considered a visible sign for something invisible that has happened.

For some Christians, the proper method of baptism—immersing or pouring—isn't worth debating; for others it's very much worth debating.

Baptism in the Bible

The Bible isn't much help in settling the debate over immersion vs. pouring. The English word 'baptize' comes from a Greek word which can mean either immersing something in water or pouring water over something. Some people, however, will claim that it means one or the other in order to support their own position in the debate.

Some immersionists say it's obvious that Jesus was immersed because the Bible says he came up out of the water at the Jordan River. Pourers respond by saying such wording only means Jesus was standing or kneeling in water and climbed out of the river onto the bank, like we say someone comes up out of the creek or the bathtub when they were never fully immersed.

The Bible isn't much help in deciding between believer-only or infant baptizing, either. Those who reject infant baptism in support of believer-only baptism say that all recipients of baptism mentioned in the Bible were adults. Baby baptizers respond by saying we don't know that for sure because in at least three passages (Acts 16:15, Acts 16:33, 1 Corinthians 1:16) we see entire families being baptized. Those families very well might have included children. Besides, plenty of Christian traditions developed after scriptures were written, begun by early Christians and passed down through the centuries. History does indicate that Christians were baptizing infants within the first couple hundred years of the new religion.

Ironically, it may very well be that neither having water poured over one's head while standing in a church building nor being immersed is an accurate reflection of how people were baptized in Jesus' day, or for the first few centuries of Christianity. Early artistic depictions of Christian baptism, including images of Jesus' baptism, show the recipient standing or kneeling in running water and having more water poured over his or her head.

Testimony to God's Grace
Cumberland Presbyterians believe that baptism testifies to God's grace. Grace is a blessing, something that is given and cannot be earned. Baptism, then, is about what God does and not about what we do. Therefore, we baptize infants from Christian homes. Sure, the baby doesn't choose to be baptized, but baptism isn't about us, it's about God. Parents do a lot of things for their babies that the baby wouldn't choose.

When a baby is baptized, Cumberland Presbyterians believe that God is promising to love that baby until he or she is ready to hear God's call to enter into a personal relationship with God through Christ. The baby's parents and the congregation are promising to raise the baby in the faith so that he or she will be ready to hear and answer when God calls. The baby's part in baptism is simply to receive this sacrament as a gift of love and grace.

Baptism makes a person a member of the Christian family, but not a member of a particular congregation.

Cumberland Presbyterians baptize by pouring because when we read the Bible (Acts 10:45, for example) we see the Holy Spirit descend upon persons, pouring over them and their

Notes:

Notes:

lives. Scripture often calls this a baptism of the Holy Spirit. No scripture says anybody is immersed in the Holy Spirit, nor does scripture say anybody decides or chooses for themselves to be baptized by the Holy Spirit; baptism is something God does to us.

Cumberland Presbyterians also baptize older persons—children, youth, or adults—when they make a profession of faith, as long they have never been baptized. The sacrament still represents the Holy Spirit pouring over that person's life, regardless of the recipient's age.

Re-Baptize?

We do not re-baptize anybody because our Confession of Faith (5.19) says baptism is to be administered only to those who have never received it. We do not re-baptize those who don't remember their infant baptism because we believe baptism is about what God did, not what a person experienced. We believe that God marked that child and promised someday to call him or her to salvation. To re-baptize a person upon his or her acceptance of Christ is to say that God didn't keep his promise. Nor do we ever re-baptize someone who was baptized when older, because we believe baptism marks a person as a member of God's family and once we belong to God, God never lets us go. Communion is the repeatable sacrament. Baptism is the "one ride per person" sacrament. Because baptism is about what God does rather than what we do, all it takes is once.

Salvation through Baptism?

As important as we believe baptism to be, Cumberland Presbyterians do not believe anyone is saved by baptism. It's a sacrament and a very important part of the Christian life, but no one receives eternal salvation simply by being baptized. You only receive that by answering God's call to form a saving relationship with God through Christ. After that relationship is established, you can't help but want to live a Christ-like life. The flip side of this belief is that nobody is automatically doomed to hell just because they weren't baptized before they died.

So, Cumberland Presbyterians rejoice when parents present their children for baptism; and we rejoice when youth or adults hear the call to receive this sacrament and profess faith in Christ; but we also recognize that baptism is not primarily about that baby, or that teenager, or that adult. Baptism is first and foremost about God and what God does.

Theological Underpinnings

This lesson presents Cumberland Presbyterian doctrine on baptism as contained in the Confession of Faith sections 5.16-5.22. Unfortunately, some Cumberland Presbyterian ministers and elders disregard their ordination vow to abide by this doctrine. If your church is one in which official Cumberland Presbyterian doctrine has not been taught and official Cumberland Presbyterian practice has not been followed, there may be some differences between what you find in this lesson and what you and your students have seen in church. You might want to talk with your pastor about why your church practices things differently so you can have an answer when students ask.

One of the most important things to know about what Cumberland Presbyterians believe about baptism is that we do not say, 'We're right and everybody else is wrong.' So, although we baptize babies and baptize by pouring, we do not say that Christians who do otherwise are wrong. Thus, when someone joins a Cumberland Presbyterian congregation no one says he or she has to be re-baptized our way.

The main theological point about baptism that you need to make in leading this lesson is that Baptism is about what God does, not us.

The snacks, the fountain, and the connection between the water games and baptism are not overtly mentioned in the lesson. The hope is that these all will subconsciously help students focus on the idea of water, which is the element used in baptism.

Applying the Lesson to Your Own Life

If you grew up Cumberland Presbyterian: What do you remember being taught about baptism as a child? Were you baptized as an infant? If so, did your parents ever talk about your baptism and what it meant? If not, why do you think you weren't?

If you grew up in a denomination other than Cumberland Presbyterian Church: Did you adopt the CP doctrine of baptism when you joined a CP church, or hang on to the beliefs from the church you came from?

If you didn't grow up in any church: What did you think about baptism? From where did these ideas come? Did you have to re-learn or drop any ideas about baptism when you joined a

Notes:

Notes:

church and made a profession of faith?

As you prepare for this lesson, watch for baptism symbols in movies and TV shows such as characters passing through water or under falling water to mark a time of transformation or beginning a new journey. Do you think such symbols are intentionally included by the writers, or is the idea of baptism so ingrained in us that such symbols show up subconsciouslsy?

The Lesson

# Get Started (15 min)

Get 'em Thirsty

Have plenty of salty or dry snacks available during this meeting. Encourage your students to eat them, but do not allow anyone to have a drink. The purpose is to make everyone thirsty and therefore better appreciate the surprise of a cool drink of water at the end of the lesson.

Fill it Up and Refill

Hide your water squirters and trash bags outside before the meeting. Divide students into pairs and have each pair decide who will be the "supplier" and who will be the "collector." Use those terms without explaining them. If you have a student without a partner, you'll need to participate as well.

After these roles have been decided, lead everyone outside. Have the collectors stand with their backs against a wall or shoulder to shoulder in a straight line. Give each collector a trash bag or poncho and an identical cup.

Line up the suppliers in a straight line, shoulder to shoulder, about six feet away facing the collectors. Give each a filled water squirter. Explain that on your "go," the suppliers are to try to get as much water as possible into their partners' cups in two minutes. Suppliers may not move any closer to the collectors. Say, "Go."

When time is up or all the suppliers' squirters are empty, use the measuring cup to measure the amount of water in each collector's cup. The team who collected the most water wins.

If you have enough time, these two winners now become competitors in the second part of this game: Refill.
Give each of them a trash bag / poncho and an identical cup. Choose a third student to blindfold and handle the hose. The hose handler's job is to stay in one place (he or she may not move his or her feet) and spray the hose wherever he or she wishes, changing direction at will. The two players compete to be the one who catches the most water in his or her cup in two minutes. Everybody else's job is to watch the fun and try to stay dry. Say, "Go," and get out of the way. After two minutes say, "Stop" and turn off the hose. Use the measuring cup to see who wins. Use the beach towels for the two players.

Congratulate everyone and go back inside for the rest of the lesson.

Fill It Up Indoor Version

If you don't have appropriate outside space or if you're leading this lesson in extremely cold weather, follow the directions above but stay indoors and have the collectors stand or kneel on bath towels. Play only Fill It Up, and skip Refill.

If space, time, weather, or something else makes these activities impossible, check out Rainstorm Brainstorm in the sidebar.

Listen Up (25 min)

Learning about Baptism

Say: *Most Protestant denominations recognize two sacraments: baptism and Holy Communion. A sacrament is a vehicle for God's grace. That is, an officially recognized action through which God's grace always comes to those engaging in the action. So, most Christians believe that God is always present in the sacrament of baptism.*

Notes:

Baptism did not start as a Christian thing, but a Jewish thing. Jesus, however, gave baptism a Christian meaning when he received it. The earliest Christians picked up on its importance and passed it along through the centuries to today.

Discussion Questions:
- Who here has been baptized?
- What do baptism services look like at our church?
- Who has seen a baptism service at another church? How was it different?

Have someone read aloud Matthew 3:13-17.

Say: *John the Baptizer said he was baptizing people as a sign of their repentance, so this baptism represented their turning away from their sins and turning toward God. Jesus, however, was without sin. He had nothing to repent of. He had no sin to turn from. He was already turned toward God.*

Discussion Question:
- So why did Jesus get baptized?

Allow answers, and then share the different possibilities mentioned in the background information.

Circumcision – the Old Way (Optional)

Explain in your own words what circumcision is and how it came to be replaced by baptism.

Using the background information, explain that Christians are not in agreement on the details of baptism. Then contrast believer only baptism with infant baptism, and immersion with pouring.

Use your own words or these:
Believer baptism symbolizes that a person has decided to accept God's gift of forgiveness made possible through Jesus Christ. Infant baptism symbolizes God claiming a child as his own and promising someday to call that child to establish a saving relationship with God through Christ and lead a Christ-like life. See the difference? One starts with the person's decision and the other starts with God's decision.

Say: *Immersing someone in baptism symbolizes that person dying to his or her old self and rising again with the resurrected Christ. Pouring water on the recipient's head symbolizes the Holy Spirit pouring over his or her life. Both methods indicate that the baptized person is now marked by God. Both methods can be considered a visible sign for something invisible that has happened. Pouring, though, focuses more on what God is doing.*

Say: *Cumberland Presbyterians baptize by pouring, but we do not say, 'We're right and everybody else is wrong.' So, when someone joins a Cumberland Presbyterian congregation no one says he or she has to be re-baptized our way. In fact, we don't re-baptize at all because baptism is about what God does. In baptism, God claims a person as his own, and that never needs re-doing*

Say: *When a baby is baptized, Cumberland Presbyterians believe that God is promising to love that baby until he or she is ready to hear God's call to enter into a personal relationship with God through Christ. The baby's parents and the congregation are promising to raise the baby in the faith so that he or she will be ready to hear and answer when God calls. The baby's part in baptism is simply to receive this sacrament as a gift of love and grace.*

Also explain that we baptize older children, youth, and adults when they make a profession of faith, as long as they have never been baptized. In these cases, baptism still represents the Holy Spirit pouring over that person's life.

Say: *Cumberland Presbyterians baptize by pouring because when we read the Bible (Acts 10:45, for example) we see the Holy Spirit descend upon persons, pouring over them and their lives. No scripture says anybody is immersed in the Holy Spirit, nor does scripture say anybody decides or chooses for themselves to be baptized by the Holy Spirit; baptism is something God does to us.*

Explain that Cumberland Presbyterians do not believe anyone is saved by baptism, but only by answering God's call to form a saving relationship with Jesus Christ.

Leader Tip:

The current Confession of Faith, adopted in 1984 does not expressly prohibit immersion, but says pouring "fittingly symbolizes" (5.21) baptism of the Holy Spirit. Earlier versions of the Confession of Faith (1814 and 1883) stated that baptism is "rightly administered" by pouring.

Leader Tip:

Intentionally, there have been very few scripted discussion questions in this lesson. Youth may have many questions about baptism, and they need the freedom to ask questions in their own way. For this section of the lesson, allow your students to ask anything about baptism. Don't be afraid to answer a question with, "I don't know. Let's find out together." Spend about five minutes allowing students to ask their questions and mentally process the sacrament of baptism as a group.

Now What? (10 min)

Remember Your Baptism

Talk with your pastor about having a service for the remembrance of baptism at the end of your lesson. If that is not possible, ask about including one in Sunday morning worship sometime soon. The first Sunday after January 6 is Baptism of the Lord Sunday on the liturgical calendar and is a great day to include such a service in Sunday morning worship. You can find the order of worship for this service in the Book of Common Worship, available from CP Resources.

Live It (5 min)

Distribute water to your thirsty students and as they enjoy drinking it, close with a prayer:

We thank you, God, for water. At creation your Spirit moved across the face of the chaotic waters, calling forth order and life. In the days of Noah you used water to give humankind another chance. In the days of Moses you led Israel through the water of the Red Sea, passing out of slavery and into the freedom of the Promised Land. With the water of the Jordan River, Jesus was baptized and anointed with your Spirit. With water prepared and blessed by faithful believers, some of us in this room have been baptized. We thank you, God, for water: water to nourish our bodies, water to sustain the earth, water to quench our thirst, and water to mark us as your children in baptism. Amen.

Distribute copies of 'Baby Showers: Baptism in the CP Church' to each student.

Resources used in creating this lesson: *Book of Common Worship, Confession of Faith*

©2011 Discipleship Ministry Team of the Ministry Council of the Cumberland Presbyterian Church, All Rights Reserved.

Baby Showers: Baptism in the C.P. Church

The image above shows how Jesus' baptism may have taken place, as recounted in Matthew 3:13-17. This may be how baptism was done for the first couple of centuries of Christianity: with the recipient standing in moving water and having water poured over his or her head. (NOTE TO EDITOR: I've no idea where I got this image. I'm hoping there's a freeware one like it somewhere that can be used. Let's NOT use any image that suggests full immersion.)

If you were baptized as an infant, ask your parents to tell you about that day. Who was there? Who was the minister? Check church records to find the exact date if you need to, and then mark this date on your calendar each year. Say a special prayer on that day, thanking God for your family, your pastor, your youth leaders, your Sunday school teachers, and anyone else who has helped you understand what it means to be Christian. If you've already made a profession of faith in Jesus Christ as Lord and Savior, thank God for keeping his promises made at your baptism. If you've not already accepted Christ, listen for God. Is God calling you and empowering you to accept Christ now?

If you were baptized when you were older, mark that day on your calendar each year. Say a special prayer thanking God for the gift of salvation. Have a special celebration and tell anyone who asks what you're celebrating something like, "Today's the anniversary of the day I accepted God's gift of grace and entrusted my life to Jesus Christ completely."

If you have not been baptized, spend time in prayer listening for God. Is God calling you to make a decision? Talk with your parents, a church youth leader, a pastor, a teacher you know to be a Christian, or someone else who obviously lives out their faith. Ask them about making a decision for Christ.

Keep your eyes open for baptism images in movies, TV shows, music videos, etc. These may be stuff like characters passing through falling water, characters being submerged and then resurfacing, rain pouring down, etc. Such images may be intentional allusions to baptism, especially if they happen at a moment in the story in when the "baptized" character is undergoing some kind of significant change or transformation.

Baby Showers
Baptism in the C.P. Church

If you were baptized as an infant,
ask your parents to tell you about that day. Who was there? Who was the minister? Check church records to find the exact date if you need to, and then mark this date on your calendar each year. Say a special prayer on that day, thanking God for your family, your pastor, your youth leaders, your Sunday school teachers, and anyone else who has helped you understand what it means to be Christian. If you've already made a profession of faith in Jesus Christ as Lord and Savior, thank God for keeping his promises made at your baptism. If you've not already accepted Christ, listen for God. Is God calling you and empowering you to accept Christ now?

If you were baptized when you were older,
mark that day on your calendar each year. Say a special prayer thanking God for the gift of salvation. Have a special celebration and tell anyone who asks what you're celebrating something like, "Today's the anniversary of the day I accepted God's gift of grace and entrusted my life to Jesus Christ completely."

If you have not been baptized,
spend time in prayer listening for God. Is God calling you to make a decision? Talk with your parents, a church youth leader, a pastor, a teacher you know to be a Christian, or someone else who obviously lives out their faith. Ask them about making a decision for Christ.

Keep your eyes open
for baptism images in movies, TV shows, music videos, etc. These may be stuff like characters passing through falling water, characters being submerged and then resurfacing, rain pouring down, etc. Such images may be intentional allusions to baptism, especially if they happen at a moment in the story in when the "baptized" character is undergoing some kind of significant change or transformation.

The image above shows how Jesus' baptism may have taken place, as recounted in Matthew 3:13-17. This may be how baptism was done for the first couple of centuries of Christianity: with the recipient standing in moving water and having water poured over his or her head.

Notes:

About the writer...

Andy McClung, the writer of these lessons, was born into a Cumberland Presbyterian family, was baptized as an infant in a CP church, was taught what it means to be a Christian in a CP church, professed his faith in a CP church, and heard the call to ministry in a CP church. When God told Andy that he was supposed to become a minister, though, Andy realized he didn't really know much about the CP church. A few years at Memphis Theological Seminary fixed that. Andy graduated from MTS with a Master of Divinity degree in 1994 and loved learning so much that he went back to earn a Doctor Ministry degree in 2002. He still loves to learn.

Over the years, Andy has served CP congregations in Alabama, Mississippi, and Tennessee as youth minister, stated supply, associate pastor, church administrator, interim pastor, and pastor. He has served as interim pastor and pulpit supply in churches of other denominations too, but he's never been tempted to leave the CP Church. Not only is it home for him, but - more importantly - the CP Church has the best theology out there.

Nowadays Andy lives in Memphis, Tennessee. He writes for fun and a little bit of profit (though he hopes to write for much more profit some day); preaches on Sundays; and serves as a part-time professor at MTS, teaching the Cumberland Presbyterian courses. He also serves in a variety of roles on the presbyterial, synodic, and denominational levels. His full-time occupation, though, is being husband to Rev. Tiffany Hall McClung and father to Ian and Maggie. His hobbies are many and varied, and probably of interest to no one but himself.

Since teachers usually end up learning far more than they pass along to their students, and since writing curriculum is essentially teaching teachers, Andy is extremely thankful for being asked to write these lessons. It is his sincere prayer that they draw teachers and students closer to God, through Christ, by the power of the Holy Spirit. Additionally, Andy hopes that these lessons strengthen students and teachers in their Cumberland Presbyterianism.

Editorial supervisor is Elinor Brown. Copy editing by Cindy Martin. Electronic processing and incidental layout by Matthew Gore. **Faith Out Loud** logo by Joanna Wilkinson. Produced for the Discipleship Ministry Team of the Ministry Council of the Cumberland Presbyterian Church.

www.ingramcontent.com/pod-product-compliance
Lightning Source LLC
Chambersburg PA
CBHW080734230426
43665CB00020B/2736